REAL ESTATE

The Complete Guide to Successfully Invest in Create and Sell Non-fungible Tokens in the Virtual Property

(The Real Book to Become a Millionaire Real Estate Investor)

Charlie Reynolds

Published by Jordan Levy

Charlie Reynolds

All Rights Reserved

*Real Estate: The Complete Guide to Successfully Invest in
Create and Sell Non-fungible Tokens in the Virtual Property
(The Real Book to Become a Millionaire Real Estate Investor)*

ISBN 978-1-7780579-0-8

Legal & Disclaimer

The information contained in this book is not designed to replace or take the place of any form of medicine or professional medical advice. The information in this book has been provided for educational and entertainment purposes only.

The information contained in this book has been compiled from sources deemed reliable, and it is accurate to the best of the Author's knowledge; however, the Author cannot guarantee its accuracy and validity and cannot be held liable for any errors or omissions. Changes are periodically made to this book. You must consult your doctor or get professional medical advice before using any of the suggested remedies, techniques, or information in this book.

Table of Contents

Introduction

The next chapters will cover the essential things you need to learn to start investing in real property. It is a fantastic way to earn money while also enjoy a lot of fun simultaneously. There are so many choices you could make with this investment that you can easily diversify your portfolio while staying in the same market.

This guidebook will spend some time looking at how you can work in the real estate industry. We will discuss the steps to begin your career in this field as well as how to get the money your investment requires, how to work with a property management company and an estate broker and how to choose the lease that will best suit the property you are investing in, many more. There are numerous aspects when working in the real estate industry and the majority of them are based on the kind of property you plan to utilize and whether you plan to turn it into a rental property, or lease it to other people. This guidebook will assist you regardless of what you intend to accomplish with this investment.

When you're eager to put the money you earn and earn a profit on this market of real estate be sure to read this book and discover everything you need to know to start now.

There are many books about this topic that are available, thank you for choosing this one! We have made every effort to ensure that the book is filled with as much helpful information as we could, so please take advantage of it!

Chapter 1: What's a It's A...

Making the transition to real investment with the right mindset is a must right from the beginning. One of the mistakes novice investors make is to treat investing in real estate as gambling or as a job they do not wish to pursue. It's an enterprise. The quicker you get your head over what it means to be a part of and manage an enterprise like real estate investment and the simpler it is to implement.

The success of a business depends on its reputation. Have you noticed the signs that are placed on the streets which are handwritten with the words "we buy housesof regardless of conditions?" You probably have seen one or two. You may have thought that somebody else had taken it to the next level with the use of stickers and numbers for their own signs. It's important to note that these signs are positioned on the roadsides in a variety of cities due to the fact that these individuals have been taught at seminars that you can be wealthy quickly by putting up some signs that advertise the real estate investing.

The drivers of automobiles, don't take note of these signs, and even if they do, they scoff at the signs, not being able to believe that the person putting up a sign that appears to be authentic. How you conduct yourself as well as how you behave and the way you present yourself to people will determine what they think of you.

Your reputation must stand when questioned regardless of whether you're looking to market an investment or flip houses. You may also need to let properties. If you do not approach the real estate you invest in like an investment then it will be a victim.

The idea of investing in REITs and real estate investment organizations must be viewed as an enterprise. It could be a side job, but you are working full-time and bringing money home to pay the costs. But, it is important to remember that above all else, it's an actual business.

You're engaged in making money using money. The way to do this is real estate, not mutual funds and the hard working at the job you are currently in.

credit history and reputation

It is possible to have an unresolved bankruptcy on your credit report and still enjoy a good reputation? There's been a stigma attached to bankruptcy. People are viewed with suspicion when they are in a tough spot. However, many celebrities and businessmen have had to declare bankruptcy due to poor choices in the recession.

Don't think that your past is a threat to your reputation in any way. If you've had a difficult period that required you to file for bankruptcy or file for bankruptcy, let the transformations in your life demonstrate that you are not going to let that to occur again. Don't deny it or cover it up.

The banks and lenders are likely to be able to see your credit history and score. They will want to ensure that your reputation is strong enough to manage the venture you are starting. You should try to eliminate any negative marks that might affect your credit score, so the possibility exists. It is mentioned due to the fact that it takes 10 years for it to disappear from the credit score. In that time you may want to establish a new company and will notice that your interest rates are bit higher.

In addition to the negativities, you must be aware that you should be sure that your credit history is correct. If you find things that don't belong under your name, or information which is between 7 and 10 years old and is not helping but is affecting your credit score, you need to get them eliminated.

Each time you apply for an additional loan, your credit history is scrutinized. You could be in a position to buy a rental property on your own or borrow against the property using an unsecured loan, and therefore your credit history is important.

When you think about investing in real estate as a business option, you should also be aware that banks will view you as an individual who comes to borrow money, even having a corporate identity for your property investment. This may not be fair however they are able to.

The banks need to know that the person who owns the business is planning to repay the loan, regardless of whether it's via personal or business accounts. There are ways to avoid this, like incorporation to gain tax advantages and making sure the personal account is not merged from your business accounts.

A tax accountant who can aid you in the legalities of investing in real estate is crucial in your accomplishment. This is another way to think of your real property investment as a commercial decision , not a one-time full-time job is something you "have" to complete.

How do you find a real Estate Accountant

You could search the Yellow Pages to find an accountant, but will this really serve your needs? No. You need an account that is educated on the law of real estate. They do advertising on the Yellow Pages however, you'll need more details than the phonebook will provide.

Consider instead:

Joining an investment in real estate locally club. With the help of this club members have access to a variety of experts and accountants for real estate.

Check with local banks and request the names of real estate law firms.

If your broker is already in place, you can ask to your agent if they are aware of a trustworthy person.

Networking is among the most effective ways to locate a real estate agent.

Don't forget to contact your tax accountant at present.

Some accountants have a deep understanding about different aspects of accounting however there are accountants who devote the majority of their time managing just personal accounts. Your accountant might be knowledgeable about investing in real estate as a form of business and might help to set up your business and also take deductions. If the accountant isn't able to help you, they might be able to suggest an individual who could.

On the internet, you can find accountant websites. These websites, along with other professional-oriented registration sites will inform you which accountant is who, their field of expertise, and whether their paperwork is up to date. Accounting professionals are certified, which allows them to continue their work. It is important to ensure that the accountant you choose to use is in top standing.

Reviews will aid you. Reviews from clients help you sort through the many accountants that are available and can let you know if one is more reputable than another. reputation.

Chapter 2: Real Estate Warrior - Why You Need One

The Internet

Do the Internet mean the end of real estate agents? Since other professions have also embraced technology and the World Wide Web - travel agents, encyclopedia salesmen music stores financial advisors, Blockbuster all of them have to shift their focus or update their skills and expertise to be able to be successful and survive (or not be able to survive) in the new environment of Internet. Consumers today are lured by the immediate gratification of the internet's ability to deliver information online streaming entertainment and the ability to access basic necessities (food and drinks, transport) by pressing one button, and further up the order of their needs to have become self-actualized via the Internet. In a world where the interaction with someone else could be detrimental to your ability to finish a task, people are choosing to stay away from the hassle by taking care of it by themselves.

As an Real Estate Warrior, this should be acknowledged and accepted as a element in building relationships. often people simply want to be to themselves! Wait. What? Real estate has been founded on the belief that we have to offer our expertise and time to the uninformed and unaware public. It's back to the concept of time. It is crucial for those who are the Real Estate Warrior understand that it's not only their time that is being utilized, but it's also their clients' time being utilized. This concept is often ignored to the agent who is selling real estate; however , the Real Estate Warrior takes pride in respecting the time of their clients as well as their own.

I'll tell you when I'm just wasting my time

It is important to note that the Real Estate Warrior is built to last a long time building and sustaining the trust of their clients and establishing a relationships that are mutually beneficial to both of the parties.

Like any healthy relationship, there should be boundaries that are respected and enforced by all parties. A Real Estate Warrior understands this and sets these boundaries to ensure the success of the relationship as early as the very first interaction with the prospective client. Note that I said potential client in the initial contact this is the term used to describe the buyer or seller of the home is. If a company does not speak this word out loudly and it is the real Estate Warrior who decides on whom they will work with and with whom they do not work with! !

A majority of real estate agents collaborate with anyone (and I do mean anyone) in the short-term. The short-term term is the act of showing potential buyers a selection of houses before they have any kind of mortgage pre-approval from a reputable lender. Real estate agents explains the necessity of this period because they are "building trust" and "establishing the relationship" with buyers, without pressure or frightening them away. I would call this BULLSHIT This is a big deal! The real estate agent is aware that if they don't cooperate with this buyer, an agent else will - keep in mind that it's a zero sum game - and they're willing to gamble their most precious asset (whether they realize they are doing it) to spend some time and energy with someone that could or might not be able an apartment.

It's only when some time has passed that an agent can figure out whether the buyer is and willing to buy a house. This is the exact time frame which the majority of Real Estate Warriors NEVER encounter with! This is because the Real Estate Warrior - out of respect for their profession and their time as well as their client's time - will be certain that the purchaser is prepared and willing to buy a house prior to showing them any house.

A Real Estate Warrior cultivates relationships starting from the very first interaction and starts to build an ongoing, positive relationship. Wait. What? The conventional wisdom of real estate is that when you are pushing too hard, the client will switch to another agent . After all, at present, there are 1,300,000 REALTORS across the United States - the most since 2007-2008 (when the bubble broke)! The conventional wisdom is that agents must follow the advice of their clients and let clients to control the procedure. If you don't , the client will be to another agent. If you cause the client to be angry, the client is likely to go somewhere else. If the customer doesn't appreciate what you say regardless of whether it's truthful and accurate the client will switch to another company. You'll lose the sale and you will not receive any commission, and you will not be able to earn an income and be be successful which is why I call it"BULLSHIT!" !

Okay, now after we've explored the myths and falsehoods that are pervasive in the business environment and the tenets of an apparent outdated business model, let's talk about the reason you must become an Real Estate Warrior and WHY your clients should have the services of a Real Estate Warrior. It's important to note that I have said Real Estate Warrior NOT a real estate agent.

An agent for real estate, to either the seller or buyer is an essential evil. If they were able to take on the task by themselves, they would. From the first moment of contact each real estate professional is an agent for real estate to the buyer and seller. What happens in the first interaction can help buyers and sellers identify who is the Real Estate Warrior - if you're one. The buyer decides the who, what, when and what the procedure will be.

THE CLIENT IS CONTROLLED CONTROL

This is a complex concept to grasp, but to accept for many real estate agents. What is the best way to ensure that the client is in control? We have the knowledge and expertise and experience, aren't we? It's possible however, the client is able to access data (remember "the the book") immediately because of technology like the World Wide Web. If the client doesn't trust you , no words or actions will improve that relationship. In reality, when

15

clients become an agent in real estate but then vanish after just a few shows and don't respond to messages and the professional struggles to keep in touch with the client (i.e. the conversion rates from prospective to customer) in the event that they disappear - it's not the client's fault.

The modern client isn't required to see an agent. The capability that the Real Estate Warrior to use their expertise to establish an effective and long-lasting relationship doesn't "make" customers to do anything, but will help the client be aware of the things that are best for their (the client's) best interests as well as "WANT" to collaborate together with the Real Estate Warrior. The notion"want "want" is essential in establishing a positive, long lasting relationship because those who are eager to complete a task will be more likely to know why it is crucial to their achievement. Understanding the needs of the client is as important as earning their confidence - and in actual fact, knowing their needs will improve the trust they place with them and their Real Estate Warrior.

Given the present circumstances and the ability in internet, Internet The question which is begging to be answered is "Why do I require a Real Estate Agent/Warrior?" The answer to this question lies within the field it self. Like any other type of business, depends in the capacity to portray its clients as having people who have the ability to know and perform things others can't accomplish for themselves...or are unable to be able to do themselves. There is a concept in the real estate industry that learning more knowledge aids in increasing your income, and it is widely accepted in the real estate sector. The belief is that the more training you get regarding property "stuff" is the greater amount of money you'll earn as you'll be more at serving your clients and the more you can serve your clients , the more reputable you will be, and the more positive your reputation, the more people are likely to want to use your services. It's quite straightforward and simple, does it not? This is a good illustration of the fundamentals of an industry that tries to differentiate its employees from the the population. Real estate is intended to be an alien concept with its own unique culture as well as its own language, ethics, and principles . It is the foundation for why"experts "expert" is required to lead the unsuspecting buyer through the mazes, bushes and dangers of a real estate transaction, and to bring they safely into the end area so that the buyer will be able to enjoy the glory of their purchase or sale. ....Wait. What?

This idea of exclusivity adds value. But it is the quality of this value that is crucial - would you buy an expensive diamond with a defect in its clarity, caret or color? Most likely not! In the world of real estate, there are many agents with serious shortcomings who receive business on a daily basis. These agents perform the minimum, are not well-informed and even less have a grasp of the laws and regulations and have no control over the process of a transaction since they can only complete a hand full of transactions per year. Also, the customers pay for a tourist or a hobbyist and not an actual estate agent and certainly not a real Estate Warrior.

Not all agents are the Same and their length of time as a REAL estate agent does not mean that the agent is successful.

A Real Estate Warrior brings professionalism and knowledge along with warmth, compassion kindness, friendship and warmth to any relationship that is maintained. The client is wrapped in a secure hug that makes the client feel comfortable, loved and appreciated all through the process and even after it is completed. The reason a client should have the services of a Real Estate Warrior in their area is to experience the apex of real estate and to bring the vision to life with the actions and efforts of you as the Real Estate Warrior.

The old saying "You are what you spend" is never more true than in the real estate market. The majority of people don't possess a crystal ball in their possession and can't accurately predict the future. Some seem to be quiet or too focused on predicting what will happen to the planet. There are many people who fear for the future, and do their best to predict the outcome. When it comes to real estate just like in the real world there aren't many guarantees which is why the Real Estate Warrior is there to answer client worries, questions and anxieties to help clients make sound decisions. A Real Estate Warrior or just an agent in real estate could make a huge an impact on the course of the transaction, and also the outcome of the real property transaction.

Chapter 3: Investing Tips If You Work

The first-timer should never stop their full-time job. There is still money needed to cover your expenses. Sure, you have money you believe you could make use of But what happens in the course of a month or six months when the yield on your the investment isn't enough to pay for the cost of your household as well as any mortgages you have? One of the most costly errors is to take a leap of faith into a new job only to find that everything goes wrong and result in the total reduction of the savings. Certain experts will advise you that you should make the move or the security you've built up is going to hinder you from making your new venture work. If you're the one percent of people that this concept is suitable for you, then great. But the majority of us aren't. You require the safety net of cash coming in, and won't push as hard if you're always concerned about your the money.

Instead of seeing your job at work as a problem, consider it as a chance to reach your goals when faced with challenges. The pressure you exert to manage everything will increase your sense of devotion to the things you want most.

Here are some ideas to invest in real estate if you are employed:

Make a list of your goals.

Learn the skills you need to be successful.

Attend seminars on your day off or on holiday days.

Create a network through your company.

Choose the most effective route to take in investing in real estate.

Consider the amount of time you are required to spend.

Begin with a modest home.

Accroît the number of properties with each achievement.

Always make use of your network to assist you.

Goals keep you alert. They help you stay focused and encourage forward. Without goals, you're only left with an idea of what you'll do to earn money. They are achievable even when you work for another person.

Earning and working give you the opportunity to take classes in real estate investment or attending seminars and even reading books on real estate similar to this. While studying, you can learn the mistakes that others have made and then set out a plan for making your business venture successful. you'll never have to worry about money since you'll still earn money flowing into.

Numbers 4 and 9 work together. First, you will create networks. You will build connections and friendships which could prove useful when you're ready to launch your own business. For instance, you may already have an estate attorney as a customer and have sold them an SEO website and a website (or whatever job you currently gives you). Within the space of six months, you're now ready to implement your plan, and you arrange an appointment at the office of your client.

The client recognizes you because of the service you provided to them and assists you with questions regarding real estate law for free. This is how you establish a relationship through your current job , and later utilize your network to assist you in achieving achieve your goals.

Not only are you able to build a network, which is going to be explained in more details in the future, but you also can utilize this network to work out the specifics. Which investment in real estate is best for you? After speaking to an agent in the field, a an attorney for real estate, as well as a broker who is members of the network you'll get a better understanding of the type of investment that is most effectively for your needs.

One thing you can't feel you have enough time for , yet some find an opportunity to accomplish it: time to accomplish their goals. You're aware of the number of hours that are included in a single day. You also know the number of hours in a day are spent doing other tasks. Before you go on, there's an exercise routine you can take part in:

Note down your daily schedule.

How many hours of rest did you manage to get?

When did you start your morning routine?

What number of minutes or hours were you on Facebook?

Did you take an opportunity to take a break of ten or fifteen minutes?

Did you have half an hour or an hour to eat lunch?

If you take the time to write down everything you accomplished in a single day, it's incredible how simple to find the time to spend five minutes or 10 minutes here and there, which you could devote to research or creating an exciting new offer.

For example, if have an hour-long subway ride What are you doing while you're on the train? Are you studying a book, gazing at social media sites, or learning about real property investing? The time is there when you search for it.

Studies on sleep show that adults need seven to eight hours rest each night. If you're getting less than 8 hours sleep it is time to alter your routine. If you find yourself awake every hour during the night, you have to think about the ways to rest better. Time loss generally, starts by sleeping, or not getting enough rest while trying to fall asleep or sleeping too much. sleeping well.

It's not even a thing that says you have to purchase 10 houses, flip them within 30 days, and then earn millions of dollars on each home. This is a great idea however if you're working to earn an income, like most people are, then it is best to start with a small amount.

Make a plan to earn an income of $1,000 in the first month of your real estate investment. You can increase the amount of money you earn every month until you're making more than you've set in your goals. Maybe all you require is an extra $1,000 each month. The idea is that you need to begin small, and start with real estate investment that is a good fit into the time you allocate to your new venture. Once you have begun to grow the amount of money you earn, you could begin to cut down on the time you are working at your current job or stop working altogether.

Here are some guidelines to keep in mind:

You should have six months of bills in your account before you leave from your job.

At least $2,000 of an emergency fund to cover car or home repair.

Set realistic expectations for real estate investments.

If you are able to adhere to these three bullets, then you are able to move on from your current job. Take note of the six-month period of expenses and the emergency account are added to a retirement account that is solid and additional cash to fund your real estate investment plan.

If you have six months worth of expenses, and $2,000 in your reserve fund for emergencies, or you plan to use the $100,000 from an account for retirement or the equity from your home you live in, this strategy isn't going to be successful.

It is essential to have money for investment. The investment money you have could lose and not have begin your financial journey from scratch or, even more losing your home or car and even your job.

Be shrewd. Make investments with money you are able to afford losing. Utilize your network.

Chapter 4: Which Kind of real estate should I Consider Buying? Existing Homes Versus. New Construction?

I'm not going to buy another house. I'll tell you the reason. My first real estate purchase was a brand new construction. It was a great educational experience. One of the most valuable lessons I learned was that the price of a new house isn't the same as the cost of a new house. Typically, the cost of a brand new house is based on the construction and land. But what happens to all the other things that are not included in the cost? I'm talking about things such as window blinds, appliances and so on. I'm talking about items like garage door openers as well as a security system and an irrigation system. The list of possibilities goes on and on. It's like purchasing a new automobile. The new home is the basic version. You'll need to shell out extra money for improvements. If you buy these upgrades through a home builder, you should be prepared to pay for premium prices for inferior materials. It's not a reason to be angry about the builder due to this. It's business, and business is about making money. Overall, you'll do better at coordinating any upgrade yourself. As time passes, you'll create a good database of business contacts which will be beneficial to you when you purchase future properties. Establishing a network of trustworthy low-cost maintenance contractors is crucial when it comes to building a successful real estate industry.

There are many other reasons why I prefer not to build new structures. Land settles with time. While modern techniques for foundation construction can reduce the likelihood of foundation issues due to settlement, the risk exists. Furthermore the construction process is more expensive than older homes generally. Modern materials and brand new floor plans are expensive. Design, architecture and marketing costs are considerably more expensive. If you buy an existing house those costs are borne by another person.

While I would prefer purchasing older homes rather than new ones however, the age of the house is still a major factor. The ideal home is between 5 and fifteen years old. If you choose this age period, you can purchase an older home that has a contemporary floor plan, but without having to pay the price of a new house. A modern floor plan is vital. The modern-day people are trendy. People are drawn to what's trendy, hip and fashionable. In the present, among the top coveted bags for women is Michael Kors. A small bag that houses an incredibly small purse and the lipstick tube is priced at more than $300. The majority of people choose homes in the in the same way. When granite counter-tops are trending and people want them, they will. If carpets in beige are trending the people will be rushing to lease your house in the event that they have carpets. When every building company is building 4 bedroom homes with 2 bathrooms the reason is because this floor design is in fashion! Keep up-to-date with the latest trends in the world of floor plans, lightning, as well as interior design, and base your selections based on current trends. When you choose homes five to fifteen years old, you'll enjoy the best of both worlds : contemporary floors for an affordable price.

To aid in quick reference and to test your critical thinking Here is an overview of the benefits and disadvantages of purchasing a brand new as compared to. existing houses.

New Homes

Advantages Disadvantages

Home warranty higher cost-per-square foot

More routine maintenance issues. Neighborhood is not well-established

Long-lasting life expectancy for the major system (i.e. roof, central heat/airsystem, plumbing, electrical) The land is still shifting

Modern floor plans. Costs for upgrades and amenities are not included (i.e. sod blinds for windows, sod etc.)

Existing Homes

Advantages Disadvantages

Cost-per-square-foot lower the major systems (roof central heat/air plumbing, electrical)

Older neighborhoods Floor plans

Amenities/Upgrades Included (i.e. windows, sod appliances, sod, etc.) The warranty for your home is not included. (Note that sometimes these warranties can be purchased at an additional cost)

Foundation set up Constant maintenance

In general, I think the benefits of buying existing homes are greater than the advantages of purchasing a new home. From my experience I've been able purchase homes that are already in use at a fraction of the market value. New homes are bought at the market price. Builders aren't willing to negotiate the price they are asking because they need to safeguard the price they are asking for their other homes that are vacant for sale. Values of the homes are significantly affected if builders are willing to accept a lower cost and it doesn't make sense.

Homes that are already in use have lower costs per square foot, and features like the window shades, sod and other appliances are typically included. This reduces the time between purchase to sale, resulting in a quicker turnover and the investment funds are returned to you quicker.

Existing properties can be purchased via auctions on the internet as well as through foreclosure asset management companies, whereas new homes are bought at market value through builders who build new homes. Most of the time, the amount of income that could be earned between existing and new structures is not significant and does not justifiably justify the higher cost for brand-new construction.

I've based my personal plan around homes I have and I would recommend that you to do the same. If your purchase is well-chosen they are enduring in their value and earnings.

Chapter 5: Forms Required At Closing Formularies Required at Closing

States are different in that they require sellers to reveal any defects in their property to prospective buyers. If you live in Caveat Emptor states (Wyoming for instance) (also known as 'buyer beware states, it's the responsibility of the buyer to conduct their own due diligence and find out whether there are any known issues, like a roof leak. The seller isn't able to lie, but they aren't required to divulge the information in advance. To avoid being shocked to find out, always ask the seller and agent about any property problems and never fail to perform an inspection at the house. If the inspection of your home reveals an issue that was not reported by the seller on the form of disclosure for the condition of the property then the buyer has the right to cancel the contract and ask the seller to fix the issue, or request the seller to provide an amount of discount on the sales cost to fix the defect following the sale.

Be aware that, as per federal regulations the seller doesn't need to reveal whether a person who has HIV/AIDs resided in the home when the suicide or murder took place within the home or if a sex offenders lives near by. Megan's law requires that authorities identify sex offenders, however it is the responsibility of the buyer to look up local registry in case they're concerned.

The Comprehensive Loss Underwriting Exchange, also known as the CLUE report is provided by insurers that are part of the program. Property owners are able to request one free copy each year. Buyers can request the seller to provide an exact duplicate of the CLUE report. The report is usually utilized by insurance underwriters to determine if there are any claims from the past (within the past 7 years) that might have an impact on the price of the policy. If the report is readily available, it's advised to obtain a copy to determine the claims that have been made for the benefit of the home during the last seven years.

If you are buying a new or renovated property with new materials it is recommended to inquire about a warranty for your home. New appliances usually come with warranty from the manufacturer. If you purchase a new building where the windows, refrigerator or HVAC system fails and you need to get the repairs free of charge within the warranty of the manufacturer. The home warranty on the other hand covers the defects to the structure and materials used to construct the new or renovated home. It can be provided by the builder, or an outside party. Government-backed loans like those offered by the FHA and VA mortgages require home builders to purchase third-party warranties for their new homes in order to safeguard buyers. When you purchase the home warranty, make sure to review the section that outlines who pays for arbitration costs that are binding and could amount to thousands of dollars . They will be incurred in the event that the parties to an issue with a warranty cannot come to an agreement through mediation with an impartial third party. "Binding" implies that the homeowner accepts the decision of the arbitration, and cannot seek further legal action in the court.

CLOSING COSTS, TAXES & CLOSING

Who is the most hated tax payer? If you think that everyone can lose money then you're right! The good news is that the IRS attempts to make it simpler for the middle class however, their advertising of these tax advantages could be improved. Let's discover what ways sellers, buyers and even new homeowners can lessen their tax burdens from Uncle Sam. As always, this is not tax advice . it is recommended to consult an advisor on tax issues depending on your particular circumstance.

The retirement accounts are able to be utilized to pay for closing expenses. First time home buyers and buyers who haven't purchased homes in the last two years are able to utilize up to $10,000 of their IRA retirement account without penalty to purchase an apartment. This is inclusive of closing costs, too. This is due to the Taxpayer Relief Act of 1997. If the property is an IRA (pretax) and is not an Roth (post tax) it is still required to pay tax based upon the earnings, but penalties for premature withdrawals are removed. Be aware that you are given 120 days in which to complete closing on the property prior to when the penalty waiver disappears.

The points (prepaid interest) are used to reduce the interest rate when buying of a home. They can be taken out of personal tax. Be aware that the points removed must be from the loan of a personal residence . The total amount that is deducted must not be greater than what the purchaser made as down payment.

The loan origination cost is tax-deductible. This is a great thing since it could be anywhere between 0.5-1.5 percent of the cost of your home.

The closing costs, such as the costs for title insurance premiums as well as home inspection expenses as well as broker's commissions among others , are unfortunately not deductable.

When you have your own house you are able to deduct taxes on the property and mortgage interest from your tax-deductible income every year. The principal payment cannot be deducted since you did not have to pay tax on the loan at the time you received it, which means the principle is used to pay off the debt tax-free.

Important Notice - As of the passing of the new tax laws, starting in 2018, you can only take a deduction of up to $10,000 in tax on property from our personal income! If we live living in states that have higher property tax rates, an income deduction of $10,000 could only cover a small portion, but not all of our annually imposed property taxes.

If you are using your home as a workplace then you can take the portion of your house that is used as office space from your tax-deductible income. If you lease a unit within your home and you are able to take advantage of an depreciation reduction, however only for the cost that the unit is rented. As we discussed earlier in the Concise Reads guides, this deduction is only available to companies as an expense of business. If you did not file for an LLC as an example, you'd be regarded as an individual sole proprietor renting a home in order to have the depreciation expense subtracted from the rental income.

In certain states, first-time buyers of homes are not responsible for having to pay for fee transfer (about 0.25 percent of the purchase cost) as well as the buyer is responsible for all responsibility for paying the recording fee (to register the deed's new record) which could be up to $10 per $1,000 of property value or one percent of the home's sale cost. It could be a savings of 1.25 percent of the price paid for the home for homebuyers who are first-time buyers!

Exclusion of capital gains up to $250,000 or $500,000 Exclusion of capital gains for single-family residence in which you've lived for at least two years capital gains of up to $250,000 for individual tax payers and $500,000 for couples who are tax filers are tax-free! For more information about tax advantages you can be eligible for when selling your home, refer to the publication 523 at IRS.gov. It is important to note that the loss of value of the home in the sale process is not deductable from your tax-deductible income. Also the 1031 exchange is only available for the purchase of investment properties, not personal ones.

Make sure to help anyone who are overwhelmed by this journey and guide them move on to the next stage after having read Rich Dad Poor Dad.

Chapter 6: You'll Need Experts on Your Side

When you're doing the work of renovating there are many aspects to be aware of. While taking off old fittings and fixtures and fittings, you might discover that your home is prone to dangers like insect infestation dry rot, dampness, asbestos and even wet rot and the house needs to be strengthened due to foundations failing.

It is essential to hire an expert team that will keep you updated about the standard costs for removing this kind of issue. There is a call out fee and, when asbestos is present homes, they will have to be shut down to workers until asbestos is eliminated from the property since it is dangerous to work in a place in which asbestos is being removed. In reality, the planners won't approve repairs being carried out until the risk has been addressed.

Visit these specialist companies in your vicinity and ask for pricing lists and learn about the firms. Keep track of their phone numbers and determine which one has the fastest response time since the time you spend is your money. You'll need someone to respond quickly and be competent to handle the kind of issue.

It is expected that you won't encounter difficulties of this type however, if you're flipping houses, there is a chance that you'll encounter unexpected. There is a chance that you will need to replace rotted beams or other things taken care of because you aren't allowed to drywall your home until you have dealt with them. When you start a company that is designed to flip houses, you must have experts on your side. Therefore, visiting them prior to and knowing about their availability and time of response is vitally important.

Other services you'll require will be from professionals like electricians and plumbers and negotiating prices with them as well as their availability ahead of time could help you save time. It is also important to be aware of who is available with you in the form of a laborer during the first phases of owning the home. Laborers are less expensive and, if you contract with them, it'll cost you less as well. They can be used to remove old tiling, cutting up old flooring, dismantling bathrooms and kitchens and tearing down walls when you are confident that you have enough support and wish to open up rooms by establishing the support that is required before the work can begin.

Another professional to connect with are the real estate agents, who will soon become your buddies. They're the people you need to believe in your venture since they'll be advertising the project, so even when you think it's unnecessary to meet with an agent for real estate the coffee might actually get you some more attention in the process of selling your home. It's no longer unfamiliar with agents in the field. this will help you get the highest quality of service from them and inspire them to trust the property you're planning to sell.

In one area of the town in which I reside the area was targeted towards students, while the others tend to be comprised up of houses that appealed to professionals. So, in that area of town I had contact to real estate professionals from both areas in order to rent investment properties in the quickest time possible. accessible to students and also sell properties to business professionals when the property was available to put on the market.

The other experts who are important to know are the suppliers. They're the ones whose prices will determine the amount of profits you earn and if you can find a affordable deal on bundles of electrical appliances or kitchen appliances at reasonable prices that are of decent quality and you are able to save money. Tile suppliers and flooring manufacturers are other people should be able to establish relationships with in order to are aware of how much costs and how to benefit from the discounts they provide to make the job you undertake profitable. Also, you will need access to a business which provides skips to ensure you can ensure that, on the day you get possession of a house, you'll be in a position to take it off without delay. If permits for street construction are required check if they are able to handle this, or if it is your responsibility since it is not something you want is to have the law pull you over for having a dumpster placed on the pavement that is outside of the home you are remodeling.

In getting to know each of the experts and professionals, you will have a solid foundation to what you're doing. For instance I was able to obtain amazing prices on kitchen cabinets lighting, tiles, and bathroom suites just by getting acquainted with the sales rep of one particular company. Real estate professionals I have met with provided me with valuable information on the likelihood that the home I was looking to purchase was likely to attract the market I was looking at. I was able find this out prior to making the error of adjusting the home in the right direction for the market. That saved me lots of money. It is possible to make mistakes however, if you have professionals by your side, you're more likely to avoid these mistakes. Therefore, it's worth it to join those experts who can provide you with advice to keep your company afloat.

Chapter 7: Advantages And Disadvantages Of Real Estate Investing

Real real estate investments are able to decrease the risk and also increase the yields of large portfolios. But, like all kinds of investment real estate investments have distinct advantages and drawbacks. Knowing these factors is an essential an integral part of any prudent due diligence strategy that needs to be adhered to before making the leap. Knowing the advantages and disadvantages of investing in real estate is beneficial for you regardless of whether you decide to decide on your own or seek the advice of experts in the field.

Benefits from Real Estate Investing

Simple to Understand

If you need to evaluate the understanding and learning for other types of financial instrument like bonds, shares, stocks and so on. Learning and understanding the fundamentals of investing in real estate is more straightforward. Some financial instruments are dependent on complex mathematical algorithms as well as abstract ideas that could be a major challenging learning process for those who are new to the field.

The investment in real estate is, in contrast it is simply paying to purchase a piece of land, a property that can be touched and felt. The fact that you can feel the tangible aspects of real estate investments is among the main reasons why it is easier to comprehend as compared to other elements of financial investment that are made up of complex mathematical formulas and algorithms.

The Income and Value of a property could be Increased

How do you purchase an investment? It is purchased at a specific price, and then you hold it in the hope of selling it at a better price , and thus gain an income. The value of that stock or share you invested in is dependent on a myriad of variables that are out of your control, such as how the business is controlled, how successful it is in its operations and more.

If you do purchase real estate, the management is your sole responsibility. You cannot be in control of the demographic or economic aspects of the property, but you also have nothing to do with natural disasters as well as other actions of God. In addition to these aspects others are in your hands including improving the appearance and style of your home; fixing the roof that is leaking; deciding the kind of tenant you would like to lease the property; renewing of the lease; maintaining of the physical elements of the property, and so on.

If you take care of your property properly and take care of it properly, the potential to increase its value lies mostly in your control. Property that earns money is one of the few assets with a significant significance to the average person. The land is valuable as does the structure it sits on. is worth it (even when it has depreciating value) as does the income that is earned by the property can be valuable for the future buyers.

The growth of this income based on value is in the majority of your control. Furthermore, the earnings from the real estate property is typically much higher that the yield on dividends from shares, stocks and bonds. The capacity to enhance efficiency (in regards to income) of the property you own is entirely in your control in contrast to that of the business which you've invested in by purchasing of shares.

Real Estate Investment is a Excellent Way to Hedge against Inflation

Real estate is among the assets that fluctuate according to inflation. If inflation rises it is also a time when housing values as well as other property values rise. Although real estate is generally an excellent method to hedge against the effects of inflation, renting property is much more effective (especially the residential property) given that you are able to renew leases each year and adjust them to keep up with the latest inflation trends.

This is among the biggest advantages when investing in property to earn rental income. The cost for real estate specifically multi-tenanted properties (that are characterized by large replacement and cost of labor) is also rising as inflation increases. In reality, there are leases that contain the clauses that deal with inflation, which ensure that the rent you earn from your home is directly linked to inflation.

Properties continue to exist and Profit in Unproductive Market Conditions

If you look at the comparison between the stock market to the property market there is a clear difference in the effectiveness they operate with. Stock markets are extremely efficient, well-controlled, and governed by numerous rules and regulations that are inspected and checked. The real market, however, on the contrary, is incredibly inefficient, and there is no transparency as to the value of specific property and the strengths and weaknesses of diverse markets in operation all over the world.

These inefficiencies and differences are the primary reason behind the potential for huge profits on the real property market. All you need to do is talk to professionals in the industry who have conducted their own research (or you can conduct yourself) to find properties with high potential for profits.

Real Estate Property can be Financed and Leveraged

The market for real estate is filled with houses that were purchased through leverage and financing. Yes, you can purchase shares and stocks using the use of bank debts. But, they aren't intended for the purchase of stocks or shares. It is possible to consider the possibility of obtaining an individual loan for this reason. The purchase of a property, on the contrary, can be accomplished by using financing options specifically designed for the purpose.

The real estate investments made by way of mortgages or other financial arrangements are able to be managed and structured in so such that it is cost-effective and secure for the investor. The capability to leverage and get financing can allow you to purchase large amounts of property by investing in relatively small amounts from your own end. The outcome of this strategy will be property that will grow in value each year, as another person pays for it.

Another reason to consider this is that when you have more money to leverage, you could purchase more properties, allowing you to boost how much you own in your property portfolio, while growing the equity value of it while you pay off the loans.

In addition there is the concept of "positive leverage" is also possible which means you can boost the amount of cash flowing by taking out at a lower cost contrast to the interest rate the property is paying. For instance that your property gives you a return of six percent and you're making the payment on a loan at 4 percent, this could give you the benefit of a 2 percent increase in the flow of cash in this scenario.

Real Estate Investments Offer Enhanced diversification value You are aware of the value and importance that you can get from diversifying your portfolio. Real estate investment can increase the value of this diversification due to the fact that this type of asset has minimal or no relationship with different asset types, including bonds and stocks. This means that even if the market is experiencing a slide, your earnings from, as well as the value of the real estate you own will not be affected. In fact an upward slide in the stock market can actually boost values of your property property portfolio.

Real Estate Investing Offers Multiple Tax Benefits

A number of nations such as the US permit tax deductions under depreciation expenses. Depreciation is a recognition from the federal government to all properties that are going to decrease by the value (depreciate). In the real estate industry the depreciation cost is only in writing. This means that even if you do not spend money, you are able to show the expense as an expense. This expense can be offset against your earnings, thereby decreasing your tax burden, and there's no tax to be imposed on appreciation. There are additional advantages to tax-free real estate investment that you can discover through a conversation with your tax advisor.

Advantages and disadvantages associated with Real Estate Investing

The Investment Costs are Expensive

If you decide for investing in stock or bond, the the investment may be just the sum of a few dollars. If you decide to invest in a real estate the initial investment is likely to be at minimum one thousand dollars. The transaction costs associated with buying real estate can be significantly more expensive than other types of assets.

Additionally, the size of the initial investment will impact how much value the house that you are investing in, which makes it harder to earn gains. For instance, if you purchase a property with a low cost however, the return will not necessarily result in positive cash flow since the rent income of such property isn't likely to be large.

One of the downsides of the tangibility aspect that is inherent in the real estate market is that since it is extremely physical it is likely that maintenance costs will also pop up. Costs for transactions, maintenance and initial investment expenses, etc. They all add to the total cost of purchasing a home which means that investing in real estate will cost much more than investing in other kind of asset.

Even if you plan to leverage your investment via bank loans the margin will be significant. This is the reason there are people who have saved funds for a couple of years prior to thinking about investing in real property.

Real Estate with low liquidity Investing

If you're looking to sell your stocks and shares that you own the only thing you have to do is inform your broker to let you sell or, if engaged in trading online You can sell with the click of an icon. It is beneficial to have liquidity for this situation. However, liquidity is an obstacle when it comes to investing in real estate. It is not possible to sell your property by pressing an arrow or ask your broker to locate an investor after which the buyer will show up.

It can take a long time to acquire property, and time to sell the property. Thus, investments in real estate are generally not liquid. If you are a real estate investor you should be ready to hold the property for months , and at times, even years before you are able to sell it.

The process of purchasing property isn't easy.

Making a broad real estate portfolio is an enormous challenge. To have a truly diverse investment portfolio in real estate, you need to be able to locate your property in various strategic locations. This is a difficult task for the average real property investor. There are, however, options for investing in management companies and REITs that are nearly always backed by a diverse portfolio.

Real Estate Markets Are Inefficient

For a smart investor, with the help of experts from a variety of market segments Inefficiencies can be beneficial when profits can be large. But from the viewpoint of a novice and typical investor, the inefficiency of markets could be very frustrating.

To understand the inefficiency of markets, it is necessary to understand what constitutes an efficient market. A market that is efficient is one where the value of the asset traded is a reflection of all the necessary and well-known information regarding the specific asset. This means that the price of an asset is the actual worth of the asset, which means there is no undervaluation or overvaluation.

This is definitely not the situation with real property markets. What is interesting about an unprofitable market is that an investor who has access to information that other investors aren't is at a distinct advantage and will be able to profit on assets which are undervalued. If you're an average person, this increases the difficulties of purchasing the right property. There is a lot of research needed before settling on the best property to suit your requirements. Any mishandled decision could cause financial loss.

Real Estate is dynamic and predicting the market isn't easy.

Similar to other assets the market for real estate too is very cyclical. Real estate comes with two cycles that include the investment market cycle as well as leasing cycle. Let's take a look at both of these cycles.

leasing Market Cycle - This deals with the demand and supply for space within the property market. The quantity of space that is available in the market determines this cycle from the supply side. However, how much space required by tenants is determined by the side that is demanded. If there is a growing need for space the supply side will start to shrink, which can lead to rising rents in the market. If rents rise to a certain financial level, then it could be beneficial to build (or construct) additional space to meet the rising demand.

investment marketing cycle - It operates in a way that is different from the leasing cycle. In this case, the demand market is filled with investors who have the capital needed to invest in real estate while the other side of the market is populated by homeowners who provide their homes to meet demand. If there is enough supply for investors, the prices of property will rise. As the prices rise the more properties are put on markets to sell.

While it's true that the two cycles of real estate are not dependent on each other however, one of them will influence the other. In the case of example, if leasing market is in an upward trend, rentals will decrease. If rental prices decrease, investors who want to invest in real estate find that the costs are too high, and they stop purchasing, which leads to less capital flowing towards the markets. To bring the market back to equilibrium, the costs of property are also required to be decreased.

Timing an investment in real estate can be as challenging as timing any other market. However, you need to be aware of the exact moment the market is at to make educated decisions about your investment in real estate.

It is difficult to measure performance

In the real estate market there aren't any standard benchmarks that can be used to gauge the effectiveness of your investment or to compare your portfolio and its results with other investments. In the same way, there aren't common risk measures that could be used to assess the risk involved in your real investment in real estate. Returns and risk are simple to track and evaluate objectively in other markets like shares and stocks. Monitoring the performance of real estate can be difficult.

In the end there are benefits and disadvantages of investing in real estate. The main benefit is the one discussed earlier in this chapter, which is the ease in comprehending. When you are free of the complex and confusing mathematical and technical analysis, selling and buying of real estate is simpler. You own a portion of the earth when you purchase property. And, in light of the fact that the area of our planet isn't increasing and the population is growing at alarming rate it is impossible to be wrong in making a portion of your money to real property.

It is time-consuming and requires effort to comprehend the cycles of the market and the amount of money your home will fetch in the future and what cash flow you can expect. It's not that difficult. With the guidance from experts You can make the best choices that will meet your financial needs and the satisfaction of owning a property will never be forgotten out of your heart or mind.

Chapter 8: Choosing if A Property is Worth Its Price

If you are looking to invest in properties that are ugly ducklings, getting a property you think is worth the investment is just the beginning The next step is to decide if the property is able to be renovated in an approach that it could be a rental property that is profitable without a lot of effort feasible. When you're a first-time real property investor, it may become easy to be involved in looking for the best price and proceed without considering the entire situation This can lead to failure it is why you prefer to stay clear of this pressure whenever you can. When you've discovered a property at an affordable price, you're likely to be keeping these aspects about the home in your mind before beginning to consider making an offer.

Explore the area

Take a tour of your neighborhood. First you'll prefer a barefoot in the dirt approach to looking around the neighborhood in which a possible rental could be located in, if feasible. The details of the area will allow you to understand the kind of person who will be happy to call the area home. This can provide you with an idea of the kinds of floorplans and designs would be most effective when you look inside the home. Furthermore, this trip can help you get an impression of the neighborhood in general and to possibly speak with residents, specifically residents, about the neighborhood and the neighborhood. It is crucial to talk to residents whenever possible since they will be more likely to give an honest view contrasted with owners of properties in the neighborhood who are vested in maintaining appearances.

Be aware of the local tax rates for property: When you plan to build long-term investment properties in the area, knowing the property tax rates are for the specific area is essential to make an informed decision about the property you ultimately decide to purchase. Be aware that the tax rate at which a property is charged can be drastically different between neighborhoods, and it is advisable to verify the local rates to ensure that you don't get an unpleasant surprise in the future. Sometimes, a higher tax rate is accompanied by a better location, but or it could change randomly, but regardless, forewarned is always forearmed.

Examine the amenities that are targeted to your audience at this point, there should be a precise idea of the type of tenants you intend to promote the potential property to, if it is the kind that would eventually make your property their home. It is a simple task to look around the region for facilities that can attract this particular set of tenants. For instance, if you are planning to sell your home to young families, then excellent schools and plenty of public spaces are likely to be major selling points, whereas when you're seeking young professionals, then entertainment options and the easy access to transportation routes could be more crucial. It is crucial to find a location that is suitable for the type of renter you are targeting and more than just the house. the aim should be to build on the natural advantages of a property that is ugly duckling instead of trying to combat the weaknesses of it.

Check out the details of the area When driving through an area in the night can give you a general notion of how safe it is, you're likely to require something more specific prior to deciding to make a decision on an investment property. Particularly, this involves looking for the local rate of crime to be able to safeguard your investment but in addition to making sure potential tenants aren't concerned about getting out of the house at night. A quick visit to the police station can give all the details that you require. You should inquire about the rates of vandalism or petty crimes, as well as serious crime , too. Also, look around and see the amount of police presence is present in the area generally and do an online search for news about the neighborhood in case of.

Take a look at the employment market If you're intending to rent your home solely to college students, then the current state of the local employment market will require study also. If there are big employers in the region investigate their information and make sure they plan to stay for the long haul as there is nothing worse for a region's renters more than a declining job market. Also, it is important to be on the lookout for announcements that a new business is expected to move into the area since this type of change is most likely leading to an increase in the demand for rental properties as new residents are brought into the region that are more than willing to rent for the time being until they are getting to know the layout of the region. Don't miss out into these kinds of opportunities if you're not aware of them.

Take note of plans that the city may have. While you're looking out for what the local major corporations are involved in and what they are up to, it is good to research the plans the city has in mind for the neighborhood that have piqued your attention. Plans like this can be identified by examining the old city council meetings, as any major project requires many meetings to debate the details prior to. Anything that enhances the neighborhood is likely be for you, while anything that reduces the existing facilities could be issue.

Check for any other vacant properties There may be a few rental and for sale notices in a given area is common however, a large number may indicate that the location is predominantly an annual one and you're likely to want to stay clear of and could have more subtle problems, something you'll want to stay clear of. Additionally, the higher the number of rental units that are available in an location, the higher the possibility that your home will be vacant for a longer period of time, which is another warning sign. The small amount of rentals within a particular region will guarantee that you are not lacking renters because they have a lot of options. The less local rental properties, the more rent you can charge in addition.

Be aware of any other local aspects: Last but not least it is important to be aware of other aspects which could make a specific area a poor investment. If you're searching for properties in an area that has the potential for natural disasters, like you should examine the past records for the region and determine when the last big disaster occurred. Be aware that the longer since a major disaster has passed through, the greater are the chance that the next catastrophe season will be the one that will change the chances. Finding a trustworthy rental property is about taking a long-term view and this would render this sort of problem an unavoidable issue in almost every scenario.

Visit the property

If you've determined whether the area of the property isn't a decision-maker and that the price is fair now is the time to take a look at the property you are interested in. Keep in mind that when you're looking at ugly ducklings, it's crucial to not just examine the current state of the property is at present and not examine what you could achieve with the right timing and vision. Take note of the following suggestions for finding out if a particular property is likely to make a difference, or when it's nothing more than a pure idea.

The basics are the first step The first step is that it's important to recognize that a property that is ugly and a home that is truly damaged are usually two distinct things. A home that is ugly might possess a horrible color scheme, a poor design or an outdated kitchen however, a damaged home is one that is afflicted by serious issues down to the foundation of the house. Therefore should you schedule an appointment to visit the potential property, it is crucial to look or contractor who has an eye, to significant issues that will make the property unfit for go , including roofing problems, foundation issues or basement problems or rotten support beams floors that require more than a facelift , and the damage to major systems such as heating, plumbing, and cooling. These are all issues that even a new real estate investor isn't in a position to discern by merely examining the exterior of the property. This is why it's crucial to arrive at the first viewing with a plan.

The trick to successfully locating an ugly duckling home that could eventually turn into a rental swan is by doing the kinds of improvements that will add an additional value which will increase the amount you are able to charge rent. In other words, if you need to spend money on the foundations of the property prior to when you even begin the to make profit then you will soon find yourself stuck in a pit that you are unable to truly dig out of. In the process of creating an investment property that is successful, the most significant obstacle you could confront is the expense of renovations that can spiral out of control Don't make the problem even more common than it already is to be. Ensure that the foundations of any property you're considering is solid, regardless of the type of property you are considering.

Assess the curb appeal of the property A lot of ugly duckling homes are tagged as ugly ducklings right from the moment you look at them, as a variety of poor decisions have been incorporated to create an unflattering first impression. As a real estate investor, it is your duty to be able to look beyond the current situation and look at the possibilities that the property can offer with a fresh coat paint and a suitable landscaping. Instead of focusing solely on the present you will need to consider whether the appearance of the property could be transformed to look welcoming. Consider if the problems you're experiencing can be resolvable out or is already too much. Think about the condition of the area in general and imagine the ideal scenario for the renters you're thinking about.

Think about the overall floorplan If a house with two bedrooms and a bath could sit for months on the market in some locations, renters are likely to be pounding on the front door if it were three bedrooms instead. This is the reason why once you're inside the house you'll need to think about the entire floorplan rather than the way things are set up. Of course, you'll prefer to stay clear of the kind of work that leads to moving walls that are load bearing, but any wall that isn't essential is able to be removed at a reasonable price. You should be aware of the current trends regarding the flow of the work, but it is crucial to not let current layouts hinder you from examining what possibilities are.

Do not be concerned about flooring: when it comes to the preparation of the property for rental either ugly duckling or not flooring is always one of the first things to will be replaced. That means as long as they're solid and structurally sound, the present situation isn't an issue. If your home is carpeted, determining whether there's salvageable wood underneath is always a wise option, as you don't be aware of the decisions that were made between the time that the home was constructed and the present day, but sometimes you have a chance to be lucky. Even though putting in hardwood floors that don't exist yield a value that makes it worth it, trying to salvage the existing hardwood is always recommended since it can keep costs low in the long run since it isn't necessary to replace the flooring each when the renters are moving out.

Be aware of the kitchen and bathroom If you are an investor in real estate If you are seeking a turnkey home to rent out, then finding kitchens and bathrooms that are in good condition is essential. That means kitchens and bathrooms that nobody else is interested in are an excellent option to begin looking for properties that are ugly ducklings. In these cases you should be aware of what the basic structure of the room will appear like, and in the event that you are pleased with the design, remember that these two rooms could often be transformed into a completely different appearance by changing the appearance of a few essential elements. Although these rooms may be smaller or have a different shape than you'd like, there are tenants you can count to be reliable and don't really pay attention to the details. If you find an apartment that appears at first impression to be an issue, think about considering it in an entirely different perspective.

Think about the storage space When you are trying to find the perfect rental property the majority of tenants mention the lack or storage spaces as an enormous dissuasion. Furthermore, a home designed specifically with storage space in mind can be able to handle the issue better than those that are built later on. Therefore, when you're doing your home search, you'll certainly want to put the proper importance to homes which have this issue addressed and managed well. You can easily change colors, flooring , and take down unnecessary walls, but putting closets that aren't any is a different story completely.

Chapter 9: How Market Conditions Influence Your Investment

Many investors who are new are excited to start investing with real property. They might hear about other investors who have made this type of investment and earned an impressive amount of money in the process. However, before you invest in this venture it is crucial that you know the way it operates. The first step is to know what you can determine what the current market situation in your local area is, to help you make wise choices.

There are many different markets in property markets. There are periods when people are looking for homes, and you'll notice that the prices of homes are excessive. This is the time when you may need to think about selling a home or altering the rent to make the highest amount of money. There are also times when the demand for houses is at a low. This is a great opportunity to buy a house as you're more likely to obtain an attractive discount on the cost. The various phases of the cycle can occur all through the year, however generally, you'll want to keep an eye on the overall changes from year to year.

There are many instances that the current market conditions within the real estate market will have a direct impact on the time you can make purchases or when you're in a position to sell and much more. Every market will traverse these cycles regardless of how good the location is. There's never going to be a huge demand for houses and it is possible to enter into the situation where selling homes isn't easy. If you decide to buy an apartment during the down times and they do not reverse rapidly it is at least the possibility of using the property as rent to cover some expenses until the market starts to turn around.

However, it is difficult as a newbie to know when to start investing in the market to earn the most and also to ensure the market's cycle. Keep in mind that you're capable of considering this kind of investment no matter the kind of market cycle you're in as it will always follow a path which you can utilize for your benefit. A few of the various aspects of the economic cycle you must be aware of to assist you in making the most appropriate decisions about this type of investment are:

The peak The time of the peak is likely to occur when prices are at their highest ever. In this moment there is a shortage of homes is likely to be extremely low this is the reason the high demand drives up prices by so much. In actual fact it is often the case that there are lots of interested buyers that a single property even if not in great condition there will be more than one bid on it. If you are you are an investor, it isn't the best time to get into the market since you'll be paying more for your house than you are able to earn in the future. However, if you own a property and done the necessary repairs it is a great opportunity to sell it.

The tipping point is the moment when prices for homes are becoming too expensive while the market for houses is beginning to decrease. Prices are likely to drop and allow prices to offset the higher prices and excessive building that took place in the previous portion in the course of development. There are instances when foreclosure rates are expected to increase and some homeowners will face difficulties paying their mortgages because the mortgage payments are too high. They will also encounter some difficulties selling their property due to the fact that the value of their house is less than the amount the amount they owe and there aren't many interested buyers. The decline: This phase in the process is when the cost of homes in your area are expected to continue to drop. You might notice that you're at this point as you observe a large number of foreclosures taking place at the moment. There are many people who are afraid to buy homes at this time because they don't want to buy something that they're unable to afford. Due to the numerous foreclosures happening, there's likely to be a large amount of inventory in the market that will drive costs down further.

The bottomis the point at which the prices for homes are likely to begin to level out somewhat. This phase of the cycle will be the lowest priced of all the things. If you're trying to enter the market then this is the time when you should purchase a home or two as you'll enjoy a massive discount. Many homeowners eager to sell their home and make at least a little from the sale. There will be a large amount of property to examine and you'll be able get an excellent price. This will help you save money and make it easier to increase your profit at a later date.

The upswing to the bottom: It's not going to remain for a long time. There will be a period that buyers begin to feel more confident in the market and are likely to begin looking for homes to purchase. This can lead to increased homes sold in the region and could result in a decrease in inventory. As time passes, the cost will begin to rise.

As you can observe it is a cycle that is going to continue. It is important to know how to identify the various components of the cycle to be able to buy your property in the correct moment and then to make it available for sale in the appropriate moment to make as much as you can. If you purchase of a house in the height of the season, you'll have to pay an additional amount of money for the property and not make any money because it's unlikely that rates will increase.

Before you go to the market, it's essential to know which market area your current location is. If you find that your location is at the point of tipping, it is not the best time to purchase since prices are high and interest from buyers aren't as high. It is unlikely that you will make profits from these properties. However, if your neighborhood is at the bottom, and there appears to be more faith in the market for real estate it is possible to buy a home at a time when prices are lower and offers are attractive. The goal is at the time you make certain adjustments to the property and close by closing on the property, the market will have moved to climb or at the top, and you could profit more.

If you take the time to understand the cycle of markets and the way it operates One of the most effective methods to spot the indicators in the markets is to experience it. It may be that it's hard to master this skill in early on, but once you become involved in the market and begin to be involved in the investing process the process will become easy to determine what you need to do and when to exit.

Some investors jump out and look for an investment property at the start the most successful investors are those who know that the market will be able to determine whether they can actually receive a lower price for the property, and even if they can sell the property once they're completed. Find out the different phases in the process of market cycles, and you'll be

certain to make the highest return on your
investment.

Chapter 10: What to Look For to Find It

Once you've chosen the area you're looking to purchase, it's time to take the next step, which is to find the property. If you've already identified your target market and know what your approach will be (selling and renting) then you are in a position to begin searching for the most affordable bargain.

First, you have to be aware of where you should look. While you might think your realtor should take care of everything however, you're the person in charge of the first and most crucial investment. It's because when you're beginning your journey you may not be aware of what exactly you're seeking (even even if you think that you know).

Experience is the most effective teacher. You'll learn lots about what you need once you begin about looking at homes and their surrounding neighborhoods. You might have initially planning to purchase a the commercial properties, however you you later thought it would be much better and more suitable for your circumstances to purchase an individual-family house.

Make sure you open your eyes and your ears

As with any other aspect of life getting a good deal requires a good understanding of the environment. If you don't go to the local electronics shop and you don't bother to read their promotional materials You're likely to not learn that they're offering a discount on the stunning new TV the one you've wanted for years until it's too for you to wait.

The stories you read at the grocery store or the articles that you read in the newspaper during your morning cup of coffee, or the things you see posted on social media sites are one of the ways you can discover a great investment.

It is important to read all adverts for classifieds that appear in the newspaper or online. Take a drive around the neighborhood and take a good examine the area. Perhaps you'll find a "for sale" notice that wasn't there just three days earlier, but could disappear three days later. There's no way to find something if you don't venture out and search.

Meet locals

When you have a good idea of the location that you are planning to put your money, it's likely to be beneficial to visit the people who live there. Most likely, each area has a bar or a café in which the majority of residents are hanging out. If you're in one, you can present your card and business address to bartender, waiter and perhaps a few others.

Inform everyone about your search for a home and explain the house. For instance, you could inform people you're in search of a 3 bedroom house with a back yard. It is possible to let me know if you're in search of a home near an elementary school or near the mall nearby.

By mail

In today's technologically advanced society sending direct mail like postcards or letters at home owners is something you should think about. While it may seem like a costly process however, it's actually not. If you visit the internet and search for information about direct mail there are various services that offer low-cost alternatives.

In your letters, you must describe the person you are and explain what you're searching for. Tell them that if they're willing to consider selling their home You are always there to visit and then sit down for a cup of tea.

Of course. This process could be extremely disorienting because of the low response rate. It is possible to write 500 letters and receive only 15. However, who is to say? Perhaps one of those who replied to your message did not have a plan to sell initially, but altered his decision after meeting with you. You might have discovered an under-appreciated gem and you don't have to pay an agent to help helping you find it.

Join a network group

There are numerous real estate networking groups as well as trade associations that you could join to meet like-minded individuals. By joining these groups and participating in events will help you gain strategies and tricks from experienced investors.

Participating in these groups is also advantageous for your company since you'll be able to establish relationships with a variety of people in the world of real estate. A few of them could be able to become investors, future partners team members, investors as well as buyers.

Seizing Opportunities

What's the ideal deal for a businessperson? to buy cheap and sell at a high price Of course. If you have the coffee shop it is likely that you want to purchase coffee at the lowest price possible and sell coffee cups at a higher price. If you run the coffee shop, toy store, or a market stall selling vegetables You are only likely to make money if your profits are greater than your expenses.

Similar to selling and buying properties. For example, if the property's value is $250,000, and you can purchase it for

$200,000, you've saved some money , and you can then use your savings to make additional improvements to the property and increase its value.

So , how do you find these deals, particularly since our modern-day, connected and online world can make it difficult to find sellers who aren't aware of the worth of their property? There are a few ways to find amazing deals on property:

Foreclosures

Foreclosure occurs when the homeowner does not pay his mortgage. Imagine, for instance, that you purchase a duplex with the down payment of 25% and the bank loan you the remainder of the amount you'll need to purchase the property. This means that every month you must pay your bank the monthly mortgage installment, which comprises a part of the loan in addition to the bank's interest rate.

What happens if do not return the borrowed funds at the banks? Legally speaking, you are the owner of the property, and you are able to do what you want in it, so long as you make your mortgage payment.

However, the property isn't yours until you've paid the loan. If you do not pay your mortgage, the lender will seize the property of you (regardless of the down payment and prior mortgage payment) and you'll not be able to own the property. This occurs all the time. It's a sad and gruesome reality. When people lose their jobs or are injured or have huge medical bills to cover and they have to surrender their homes if they're unable to pay the mortgage payments on a monthly basis.

The bank will take over the home, typically with the goal of eventually selling it to the public. This is certainly not the best scenario, but it's a real and if you're looking to buy a property for a low price, this is a fantastic and common method to go about it.

If the bank buys it from the homeowner who was unable to pay loan obligations It is now a temporary owner'. In order to recover its investment consider selling the property to pay back the loan originally granted or at a minimum get a sum similar to the loan amount.

In certain regions, and especially those financially impacted, banks have a difficult time "unloading" these properties, especially due to the fact that there are several similar foreclosed homes. There is too much inventory, but insufficient demand (or the ability for payment).

If the property is held by the bank for a long time The bank will most likely be willing to accept a smaller amount than the original price. This being said utilize your negotiation skills to negotiate the best price that you can.

It is possible to see foreclosure listings on bank websites and classified ads in the newspapers and even at the sites of local government.

It is important to note that just because the price are discounted , it doesn't mean you can allow your guard to fall go. The majority of properties are sold "as-is" this means that the bank doesn't have any responsibility for the property's condition or plans to do any repairs prior to selling it. Always do your due diligence first.

If you do not want to work with banks, you could look for homes which are still in the pre-foreclosure process. Pre-foreclosure is a period when the owner has been unable to pay the loan but the notice of default' hasn't been filed by the bank. This allows the owner to attempt to come up with funds to pay the loan or decide to sell their property.

The time prior to the foreclosure process kicking off is the perfect moment for investors to submit offers. One method to speed up the process is to provide the owner with an amount that is small and then continue to pay off the loan.

While this might be, be aware that there's an increased chance that the bank won't be able to allow you to simply "take over" and may still seek to pursue the default notice. This is why it's essential to form an entire team. Your lawyer, and perhaps an accountant take a look and find a solution for you to accept the loan as minimal risk as you can.

Be cautious, and exercise your due diligence. Owners don't often leave properties due to financial issues. Sometimes, the owner is unable to make payments on the mortgage due to the fact that the property has grave issues, like environmental hazards that have recently been discovered.

Probate Sales

Another option to get an affordable price for an asset is through probate auctions which usually take place by bidding. There are always stories of dying people and leaving their estates to their close family members. The majority of the time the heirs don't want about the estate (especially when there are more than one inheritors) and so they decide to dispose of the property as quickly as they can and earn from the proceeds.

When the heirs have decided that they would like to take the estate is then sold at probate auctions. To market this type of estate, the judge has to first confirm there is a valid will from the person who died. person is valid. If it is valid, then the court will appoint the executors to take possession of the assets of the deceased and to pay any debts incurred on the property. If the property is "in the open', executors are able to sell the estate, with the assistance of probate lawyers.

Where can you locate such properties available for to buy? You can also call the local courthouse and request to speak to the clerk. Introduce yourself and request a details of all recent probate sales filed. If you've got this information, call the sales representatives and gather details regarding the properties. It is also possible to check local newspapers or look up probate sales on the internet. Be sure to know the rules of probate sales in the location you're interested in purchasing the property in, as they may not be identical.

It's as inconsiderate as it is to earn money in the event of someone's death (or for mortgages from being forced to leave their property) It's the way life is. Opportunities can come and go fast and if you do not take advantage of them, there's a large number of investors in the back who are not hesitant about investing so they can make a profit and boost the flow of cash.

Chapter 11: Making The Perfect Portfolio

This is an outline to assist you in setting up an investment portfolio isn't a hassle to manage. If you do it right, it's an excellent way to create wealth over time without a lot of effort. If you're enrolled in an 401(k) plan provided by your employer, you can connect it to an investment account you'll need to create to work for your portfolio. If you do not have an 401(k) or IRA, then you'll have to open an investing account. The ideal is to open an individual retirement plan (IRA) since this will allow you to pay the least amount of taxes that you can, as well as having the ability to take funds with no penalty until you're in a position to retire.

The process is as easy as doing a little research about various investment companies that offer IRAs , such as Fidelity or Vanguard In addition, you may be interested in the bank-sponsored investment IRA accounts, such as the ones provided through Wells Fargo. If you own an 401(k) then you'll be required to ensure it is properly transferred. Also, you will need join your savings or investment accounts with the savings or checking account for the purpose of purchasing bonds or index funds.

Choose your allocation of assets: While you'll prefer the portfolio you choose to have predominantly comprised of stocks, ideal portfolios consist of a range of investment options. At at a minimum, you're likely to need to invest some money in bonds as well as stocks. The amount you set aside for each kind of investment will depend on your investment objectives as well as your risk tolerance and the age of your. A good rule of thumb is to begin with the number 110 , then subtract the age of your child from it. That's the amount of your portfolio that needs to be invested in stocks. If, for instance, you're 30, and you are a good age to invest about eighty percent of the money in stocks. As you get older you're likely to need to shift greater percentage of your funds to low-risk investments.

Take a look at Index funds Index funds comprise a group of stocks or bonds which mirror certain segments of the market. they usually have lower fees and returns that are comparable to what you could get from bonds or stocks by themselves. The best funds to consider are ones that provide the lowest risk for moderate returns. A fund that is sought-after are the Vanguard Total Bond Market Index Fund. You might also think about a market index fund, which includes a mix of local and international stocks. This will help you be able to avoid situations where a dramatic decrease in value for stocks within one area can result in losing all your investment in one swift swoop.

If you are considering different options, you're going be able to remember that certain funds have minimum buy-ins or other restrictions. Conduct some research prior to selecting the right one for you. Just because your portfolio needs to be designed to maximize your profits and minimize the amount of work you have to perform doesn't mean that you have to take a lazy approach to establishing the details. Also, it is important to be aware that if you invest into a fund in greater quantity later , you'll usually receive better rates.

In evaluating your options it is essential to be aware of the restrictions imposed to you as a result of the terms of your 401(k). Certain 401(k)s restrict the amount of money you can access make sure you do the necessary research before selecting as they're likely to differ dramatically. Even if the final result isn't as solid as funds readily available on the open market, it's worthwhile to keep your 401(k) to reap the higher tax advantages.

Make contributions to your fund regularly and rebalance it at least once per year. Once you've identified the funds you're interested in purchasing and the investment allocation that you will begin by establishing the first step you'll want to do is establish an auto-renewing deposit that will include in your investment portfolio regularly. It is not a problem if the amount isn't much, when you consider it over a sufficient time and a couple of hundred dollars per month is bound increase. If you're in possession of an 401(k) the investment is even more crucial because your money is tax-free. If you treat your investments the same way as every other bill, you'll not be tempted to dip into these funds for any other reasons. After that after that, you'll be able to ignore your portfolio until the time to review your data. You might want to move from local and international stocks to a balanced mix of local stocks across different industries , or increase the amount of money you're placing into bonds. Whatever the reason you decide to do, you're only likely be able to do this every year at the most. When you rebalanceyour portfolio, you'll want your total allocation of assets to be the same as it was when you began at the very minimum. Be aware that if switch stocks, you'll need to factor in additional charges.

You might want to consider a target-date fund. If you're searching for the most simple investment option, then you might be interested in a target-date fund. These funds take care of all the work and split your funds into equal amounts that covers stocks, bonds and other investments. All you need to do is give them an exact date when you'd like to begin taking benefit of the cash you've made. They also adjust these ratios with time to ensure that you get the appropriate proportion of allocations, based on your age. The only other thing you'll be required to declare is your risk tolerance. The only drawback for a target-date investment is that the charges will be more expensive than other funds.

Chapter 12: Renovation: Decorate Your Home

After you have completed the renovations, you can breathe an exhale of relief as you've completed the most important aspect of your work. But don't let yourself relax because you're striving to achieve nothing less than the best. You should now check your bank account. If you've adhered to your plan, you will have a certain amount of cash. In addition to the money needed to promote and sell the property, you should be able to make a small amount of it. Use this money to decorate your home and you will earn greater profits than you earn from any other source. The majority of the time when people buy homes they want to have a little extravagance. Whatever house they'd like to have at the beginning, they will ultimately choose the one that looks fancy on the outside, and durable from the inside.

If you are planning to decorate your home, make sure to buy the things from the market. It's not only affordable, but also appealing. With just a bit of market research, you can purchase items for decorating at low prices. There are a variety of extravagant lights on the market that you can purchase at reasonable prices. The extravagant lighting and lamps provide an elegant look to the house and can attract buyers. An array of decorative items are on markets to create your house a new appearance. You can also seek out ideas from your acquaintances about ways to do more for less.

Paint is a must for a fresh appearance to your home. To reduce time as well as money complete the task yourself with a assistance of a few people or the help of your family and friends. Pick the color of paint with care as it can be one of the things that is that is noticed by buyers, especially women who are extremely keen about it. Get advice from experts in this area. Paint colors for walls like orange and aqua can help to make rooms appear bigger. The colors of yellow and red are believed as the colors of happiness and bring the same feeling for the people who live there. In the same way, certain colors work with wood tiles and others do not. These are the small things that are typically neglected by real estate developers when they are renovating the home. Small things that require little time and effort to determine can yield higher profits and help you stand out from your rivals.

The outside appearance of the home should also be considered with care. A better layout could eventually boost the worth of your home. You can give a fresh appearance to your lawn and create artwork and designs wherever you are able to. The car porch must be cleaned as well as painted. The hanging plants and chic vase that isn't expensive can be used to embellish the outside of the home. The majority of real estate investors are spending too much time in the interior area of their home in the process of renovation that the outside area is left to

fend for itself. Replace the old lighting with new ones in the event that there are no lights in the garage , or passageway, get new lights and repair them. These small details are crucial, since they will assist you in marketing your house efficiently.
Marketing and advertising

When your home is ready to sell it is important to draw the an array of buyers to locate an individual who will offer you the best price. It is essential to develop an advertising strategy can be used to get your message to prospective buyers. The first thing you must do to reach the prospective buyer to determine a price that is not just attractive to buyers but also generates profits for you. Although the majority of people hire agents and offer them an amount of money to promote their property but you can do it with no agent. It is up to your decision to work with the services of an agent. However, I would suggest that you first take a look yourself. Photograph your home. Also, the latest technology allows you to take these pictures without the assistance of a professional photographer. When you take the photos make sure to include all of the house, particularly that view of the outside from the street. Take photos of rooms, living areas and bathrooms from different angles , and then pick the angle that offers potential buyers the best view of areas of the home. I suggest you opt to a mixture of various marketing tools. You could offer an add-on to the newspaper, or put the advertising board outside of your home and in the most prominent part of the community, like a supermarkets or the main road. You could also print brochures that won't cost any money. It doesn't matter if you select one or more methods of marketing, ensure that you select the an appropriate type of images and include all the essential details about the property. Make sure to highlight the features that you believe would draw the potential buyers most.

The latest technology offers numerous ways of marketing. One of them is to make an online video of your home which provides your target public with a virtual tour of your house. Upload this video to different websites. It is possible to ask your acquaintances to do this as well. There is likely to be someone among your circle of friends who has an online site that has sufficient traffic. The option of paying a reputable site for your video isn't an ideal alternative.

Flippin" Homes

If you've taken an the integrated approach i.e. using a variety of methods to market potential buyers will eventually reach out to you. When you have been contacted by prospective buyers, you've arrived at the end of your venture. Select the people you would like to meet to negotiate the price as well as other paperwork. If you want to sell your house for the price you desire it is important to master the art of negotiations. Make Internet your most trusted source and simply read about the process. Learning a few words or lines is not bad in any way. It is also possible to read an article by Dale Carnegie "How to win friends and influence others" that won't take long.

Selling a home is about counter-offers. Make a sensible counteroffer considering your estimation of profit, the market value of your home and the offer of the buyer. Don't rush into making a your decision until you receive the offer you want. Once you've selected your buyer and the purchase conditions are agreed upon then you have to complete the documentation required for selling the house. However, the paperwork for selling your house is complex and involves legal issues as well. When you are dealing with this specific task, you need legal counsel. It is essential to have your lawyer along when you sign your contract, in addition to your family members or friends who are present. When I say presentable, I don't mean this person who appears attractive, but rather the one with extensive knowledge and experience in the transactions involved. It is always useful to create a list of documents you need, which could include a statement of settlement or other documents related to it, based on your selling conditions. Don't forget to provide the contract copy to your lawyer prior to the date of closing to make sure everything is legal. Be sure to shut off all your utilities before giving the keys over to the owner who will take them, as they were yours to keep. Give them all the keys you own, including duplicate keys.

Chapter 13: The Way to Make Money Investing in Real Estate Through Fixer-Uppers

There are many who are interested in real estate investment and are able to simply follow a method that employs the established and definitely most tried method of conducting real estate business buying homes that are listed for sale by owners in financial trouble. In these situations they can purchase distressed properties at the lowest prices and just fix them up and then sell the properties at higher rates and making an enormous amount of money. In actual fact it has been observed that people who have employed these simple methods have, in the course of time, made it to the point that they've made millions.

There are many reasons why homes in distress are put up for sale

The issue, of course, which one is faced from the beginning is discovering how to locate fixes. It's important to know that when homeowners become unhappy, it could lead them to stop take care of their homes and, in many cases, they could be unable to keep up in the payment of their homes. In addition, buyers and sellers are said to have diverse reasons what motivates them to enter investing in real estate for repair-and-renovation projects. Most common reasons are losing work or going through a divorce , or ailments; alcohol addiction could cause sellers to be distressed.

Whatever the reason why a homeowner is stressed There is no doubt that the main victim is the property that is suffering because of the lack of maintenance. The payments on it will also be delayed and the property becomes a prime opportunity to sell as an investment property. One of the most lucrative real estate investment opportunities are available in the case of fixer-uppers is homes that are in need of repair and owned by a seller who is currently getting divorced from their spouse and is unable to pay mortgage payments.

Yet, homes that look ugly and need to be repaired are actually quite hard to market. Buyers for such properties aren't willing to purchase houses that are in such poor condition. It is evident that homeowners prefer to invest their money into real estate investing into homes that do not require repairs, since the need to fix or upgrade an existing home isn't something that prospective homeowners will be looking forward to when buying a house.

It is true that most homeowners want a home that's a home, not something to put their hard-earned money into. In addition, if you're searching for fixer-uppers and have an investment in real estate, it is also necessary to be able to hire contractors that can make a house usable by doing a little amount of work. When you've decided that you need an expert contractor to repair and enhance your house, you could search for houses for sale at a bargain price.

In general, you should look for the ads with phrases like "as-is" as well as "fixer-upper" or "handyman's particular" or similar phrases that indicate that your home needs some repairs. A realtor in your area could help you find the proper direction. If you remain in this direction for long enough people will eventually realize that you're part of the fixer-upper section of real estate investing . They will reach out to you with suitable and appealing fixer-upper offers.

After you've found the perfect property and you have found a suitable property, you must know what the issues in the house are and then come up with solutions to these issues. Sometimes, the issues be a result of with financial limitations instead of requiring physical repairs to the property or even the property itself. If this is an issue, then you could receive a lower sale price for the home in question. But, remember that fixing-up homes in real estate investing is a hazard in which you must walk with extreme care and prudence since even a minor mistake could have devastating results.

The most important thing to remember is that you should first create a strong team, and then move on to the purchase of a house in a cautious and prudent way. Additionally, you must be ready to spend whatever it takes to fix your home. Once you are aware and act with these guidelines it is likely that fixing up the property when it comes to investing in real estate can bring in a lot of cash.

Chapter 14: Utilize References to Find Property In Distress

It is hard to emphasize how important referrals are to the business of real estate. Sometimes, our phones ring immediately with calls from people proposing special deals on homes they saw in neighborhoods. We have a vast number of customers who offer leads for a fee.

How do we locate our sources of referrals? They can be sourced from everyone, but our favorite are:

Service technicians

Repairman for air conditioning

Cleansing pools

Maintenance of the landscape

Roofers

Property managers

Handymen

Plumbers

We likely receive more recommendations via air conditioning (or A/C) repairmen than from any other source. Why? We are in Florida and you can't reside in Florida without AC. If you're in a bind and have no money You could do without air conditioning for a few days but once summer comes around and the heat is on the rise, it will catch the top of you and you'll be calling your local AC service.

If the HVAC system of a home has become damaged due to a lack of care it is a fair possibility that the home has other areas that were neglected. These types of houses are the ones that investors would like to focus on. Even if you reside in a colder environment, the same is especially true of homeowners that ignored their heaters.

Sandeep is our most trusted air conditioning repairman because we always have opportunities. He was one day doing work at a rental home in a fantastic neighborhood. He began talking with the landlord about the way that previous tenants had destroyed the air cooling unit. We looked at photos and were amazed at how badly the property was damaged. The reality was that it is the third time of eviction in just a year, and he was depressed. He was no longer caring for the house and allowed it to get in disrepair.

The landlord's most recent , unsavory tenants stole his outside air conditioning unit when they removed the house. It was a huge cost for the property owner. Although the majority of his issues could have been resolved with an adequate screening process for tenants and background screening however, it was his final step and he wanted to get rid of his property.

Sandeep came to us as soon as he could and informed us about the situation. We could bargain a good bargain on the rental property and we were able to pay a great referal fee Sandeep. Referrals for distressed properties can be goldmines, so don't forget about these!

Another of our favorite kinds of referrals comes from those who provide telephone newspapers and books. They see hundreds of houses along their route to work and are willing to share information to us in exchange for an amount of referral fees.

We have a friend of ours known as Christine who, prior to becoming an investor in real estate was struggling to raise three children as one parent. As a successful investor, Christine has not bought one of her properties from an agent in the real estate industry or classified ad, They have all been sourced from recommendations. The most significant lead source was a teen who was a phonebook delivery driver at night after school. He would spot For Sale signs on distressed properties on his routes to deliver and report it back to Christine. Christine would then visit the properties and assess the properties. Christine eventually purchased six rental properties this way and paid the teen for the leads he generated.

You will never have enough eyes on real property deals. Make sure to compensate for them properly if you buy an item they are referring to you.

Locate a Real Estate Agent to list MLS Properties for Lower Commissions

6.0%... The unpopular Six percentage... Six thousand dollars of each $100,000 is paid to a the real estate agent whenever you sell a piece real estate. A sum of $6000 is an enormous amount of money, particularly when you're trying to run a business that depends on every cent to make money.

We are very fond of the real estate professional Pat Glenn and he certainly deserves every cent earned, however we are investors who have funds at risk, and we need to reduce our costs as much as we can. The typical agent's risk is low if it involves the time of their clients and some fixed-cost marketing costs.

The relationship we share with Pat is one of closeness. Pat knows all the details about us such as our financials as well as our goals, investments and. We only work with Pat and supply him with regular homes to be sold, we will always seek a discount on commissions. Pat is confident that we will allow him to promote and market our property. Our commitment to Pat provides us with many benefits because he offers us specific information on the market, deals that could be made as well as lists of buyers looking for certain things.

Finding a top real estate agent similar to Pat is not easy however there's an agent named Pat in every city and town and you only need to locate him. A lot of real estate agents are between the business whenever the market is changing. Choose a person that has been around business for a while and stay clear of agents with no experience. The ability, commitment and experience are a must. Find an agent that can not only promote your properties, but assist you in making smart purchasing choices. After our third interaction with Pat we struck an agreement for Pat to market our entire portfolio for the price of a reduced commission and we saved significant amounts of money.

Establishing a strong partnership with an agent like Pat can not only save you money, but offer you the most comprehensive details about the regions you're targeting. Without the assistance of an agent, you could make a good decision However, with his advice you will be able to make better decisions.

Help the Inspectors and create an ally, not a foe

Inspections can be a bit intimidating. Why? Because building inspectors may accept or reject the work in progress or delay the issue of your certification of occupancy (CO). It doesn't matter if it's a remodeling project or a new build home, you'll run into these inspectors in the future.

Many of our business colleagues have been engrossed by these audits. A lot of their time and energy is consumed by worrying about the result the results of these tests. While these inspections are essential If your contractor has performed his work well, your inspections will be accepted... in the end!

They have both bad and good days, just like us and you. We make every effort to ensure that their encounter working with us will be a good one. We've been on jobsites of other people where we have seen the building owner of the property arguing with the inspector over the same issue, thereby intensifying the inspector's anger. This is a good illustration of what NOT to do.

If you're planning to schedule an inspection appointment, it is important to determine the inspector's name prior to when they will arrive. The city or county usually has an idea of which inspector will be coming to your location. Also, be aware of exactly what the inspector is searching for. For instance, if there is a plumbing inspector inspecting new pipes installed in a new house, typically the inspector will look for signs that the pipes passed the pressure test and if the rake or angle is accurate on the waste pipes. Be well-prepared to know what the inspector will be seeking and be prepared and ready to fix any issues that might arise immediately.

There was a building project that we built a 5000 square feet home that was valued at $1 million or more home. The construction process required many inspections , including electrical. The house, being this large required a power supply of 400 amps (this was about two to four times more than the standard house due to the size of the building and the sheer number of circuits required).

The name of the electrical inspector was John who was a kind person, but also an irritant if he chose to be. Our first encounter with John occurred when John visited us to check our temporary and underground power sources.

When we inquired of John what his most resentful pet peeves are to which he responded, "Gum on my shoe." What? The next question we had was bit more specific:

"John you, what do you find to be your biggest pet peeves when the inspection of homes?"

He laughed and then said, "Builders think they know more than we inspectors...they do not. I inspect more houses commercial and residential buildings than building contractor will ever set into. If they could just do their job properly in the beginning, I would not refuse their inspection and everyone would be satisfied! It's all the small things, such as making sure that all electrical wiring holes they make in the studs covered. It's not a lot of time to complete, but it's a simple reason to deny. After that, I must go back and spend my time away from my family because somebody did not do their job."

John did not wish to be a strict observer of details; he simply needed to get his work done quickly and be home with his family members and wife. In this way, we were prepared for his return to our final check.

We were able to ask John whether it was okay to follow him throughout the inspection to make sure nothing was missing. Prior to the inspection, we explained that we had instructed the workers to fill in all the holes in the electrical wiring but we were carrying two additional cans of filler in case they missed any. Yes, John found three holes in the drill which were not filled and we had to fill them in immediately.

We were given the 'Pass' mark on our inspection mark permit, and we were thrilled. John laughed when we told him, "Hey John it's a win for everyonebecause we were granted a pass and you didn't even get sticky gum!"

Chapter 15: Mortgages for Government The importance of knowing about Va and Fha Mortgages

Whatever your financial circumstances are it is likely that you're still eligible for mortgage loans, specifically ones that are backed by the federal government. Two of these mortgage loans can be found in those from the VA as well as the FHA mortgages.

VA (Veterans Assistance) mortgages are specifically designed to cater for U.S. veterans, or spouses who are survivors. Some things to be aware of regarding VA mortgages are:

* The guaranteed amount the veteran receives is known in the context of an "entitlement."

* The majority of lending firms provide VA mortgages.

In general, VA mortgages don't need you to cover private mortgage insurance or an initial down amount.

Because mortgage insurance for monthly payments isn't available for VA loans, homeowners will see that monthly payments are significantly lower than mortgage loans of other types.

* You can use these mortgage loans to refinance.

* You'll need to pay a fund fee (generally 2 percent of the amount of the loan) at the end of your VA loan.

FHA (Federal Housing Administration) mortgage loans allow Americans who are in the lowest income range to obtain funds to buy a house. These loans can also be provided to first-time buyers. In the beginning, FHA loans started off as loans for the government; however they've been gradually transferred to private mortgage insurance companies.

Here's a look at a few of the different types of FHA loans:

* FHA loans insured by insurance - For this loan you must have mortgage insurance,

regardless of whether you're planning on refinancing or purchasing a house. The requirements to be insured for FHA loans include healthcare-related facilities, multi-family as well as single-family homes, and manufactured homes. The loan is guaranteed to have lower mortgage expenses and monthly payments through this kind of loan.

* FHA Loans with Adjustable Rates The type of FHA loans allows the borrower to modify (increase or reduce) the interest rate of your loan for a certain time.

* FHA Loans with Rising Income This particular kind of FHA, at first, you'll be paying mortgages minimal. But as time passes and your income grows your mortgage payments will increase. In the event of rising income, FHA loans are ideal to first-time homebuyers and families that are just beginning their journey.

* Energy-efficient FHA Loans These loans allow you to cut down on your electricity bills as you're granted an opportunity to finance the installation of energy-efficient appliances to an existing or new house.

When you take advantage of this loan, you'll save energy while reducing the cost of your loan. A consultant in energy or a household energy ratings system will determine the amount of the loan that needs to be reduced.

* Condominiums FHA Loans There are many who are not keen on buying an ordinary home. If you're in this category, then you can obtain an FHA which offers the chance to buy a condo. It is also possible to take out a loan to help with the maintenance of your condominium, but only available if it is your principal residence. To be eligible to receive this type of loan, your property must have at least four units and the condominiums aren't able to be renovated from older condominiums.

If you're planning to buy or refinance your home and you believe your financial stability can keep you from getting an ordinary mortgage loan, consider applying to VA as well as FHA home loans.

Your Credit Score and mortgages

If you are thinking of buying an apartment, people usually try to secure an advance from the bank. But when it comes to loaning money the majority of banks will give money only to people with good credit scores.

If you've got a low credit history, you'll be able to obtain a mortgage loan through some lending organizations, but those credit cards (referred in the form of "bad credit loan") are available with a price. The costs and rates of interest for bad credit loans are extremely high and you may pay more than the original cost.

It's evident the fact that credit scores can affect the mortgage you take out, whether you are approved for the loan, the kind of mortgage you're offered and the amount you'll be required to pay back. Therefore, it's recommended that you check the FICO credit rating prior to applying for mortgage loans.

Five elements that affect the FICO rating are

1. Pay History - This will be comprised of any payment that was not made or was

late. It also includes the diverse types of monthly installments made (e.g. home, credit card automobile and so on.). The history of your payments accounts around 35 per cent of your score. So, if you've got an excellent credit score your credit history will likely reveal that you've had only a handful of missed payments. You also must complete your monthly installments in time.

2. Amount Due On Multiple Accounts If you frequently max out your credit cards , or have excessive balances on a diverse number of accounts, you'll have poor credit scores. But if you have a few accounts where you have a balance and your credit score is likely to be high.

3. The length of your credit history the length of credit history will help lenders to determine whether you make your payments in time and are in control of your finances. Be aware that you'll not get an immediate increase in your credit score for a account that's been in existence for a year which is well-managed. However there will be an improvement of your

credit rating if keep managing it effectively in the coming years.

4. Different types of credit - The term "credit" Types refer to car or student loan payments, mortgages , and credit cards. Your credit score will be low score if your most commonly utilized credit card is one that has high-interest credit sources for example, the credit card you use.

5. Recent or recent credit history Recently opened or newly opened accounts will impact upon your score. It is possible to open new accounts or request credit for new ones; but when you are doing this often your credit score is likely to be affected.

If you do not have the greatest credit score, but want to get mortgage loans there are ways that you can boost your credit score. Start by requesting the copy of your credit score through TransUnion, Equifax or Experian. Legally, every year you're entitled only to one complimentary copy of the credit score. However, you'll have pay for additional copies.

After the credit reports are received, go through it and determine what areas need improvement. If you discover any errors on your credit report (such as omissions, or other kinds of mistakes) contact the credit bureau as soon as possible. You'll need to provide proof.

Be aware that your history of payments account for a significant portion in your score. Therefore, you must try to avoid missing payments and always be punctual in paying your bills.

Utilize automatic monthly payment, and stop regularly closing or opening new accounts. Instead, try to improve your credit score by being responsible making use of the accounts you already have.

Questions to Consider Asking Prior to Signing your Name in the Dotted Line

A key aspects to keep in mind when applying for loan mortgages is that you inquire about the loan prior to signing your name down on the dotted line especially if you're not sure regarding your terms or conditions.

Do not be afraid to ask your mortgage lender or broker concerns, since the responses you receive will have an enormous influence on deciding the best mortgage for your requirements.

* How long does the Mortgage loan application process take? The typical process can take between 40 to 60 working days for completion However, there are instances when mortgage applications are approved in only 30 days. The duration of the process dependent on how fast the lender is able to verify your bank accounts as well as employment history, and the speed at which they are able to obtain your credit report and get your property assessed.

* What documents are needed to be submitted for an application? Different lenders will require different documents, however, generally you'll need to provide evidence of your income and assets.

What are the qualifications for the home mortgage loan? The qualifications that can help you get the home mortgage loan are assets, debts, work status credit history, income and employment status.

* What is the minimum down payment required? Although some loans require as high as 20% down payment, others require much less. You must determine the down payment first and then proceed from there. After your down payment has been done, the lender will provide you with a range of conditions and rates for loans.

* What is the annual mortgage Rate of Interest? The most efficient method of comparing mortgage rates between different lenders is to request and study the APR (Annual Percentage Rate) of mortgage interest.

* What are Origination Fees? A origination fee is an upfront fee that functions as a prepayment of mortgage interest. These fees aid in reducing the interest rate on your mortgage loan. They typically are due at the closing date by using points.

* Are locked-in mortgage interest Rates available? Yes they are. If your rate of interest isn't locked-in, it can change or increase prior to the closing date. This is

why it's recommended to opt for locked-in rates. Make sure you ask your lender about the fee for locking in or if you are able to utilize your mortgage points for lock-in.

What is a Good Faith estimate (GFE)? There's a lengthy list of costs that come when you apply to get a loan from a bank. In addition your broker or mortgage lender is legally obliged to provide you with a list of estimates of closing expenses prior to requesting the loan. Remember that advance payments are required for charges like the mortgage application and appraisal charges.

What is a prepayment Penalty? It is a clause in your mortgage contract that states that a penalty is going to be imposed if you fail to pay your loan within a specific period of time. Before the signing of your mortgage agreement, be sure that you understand what the penalties will look like, as well as the time frame for the penalty time.

* Will There Be Any delays during the Mortgage Loan application process? It all

depends on the completeness and accuracy of the information that you submit to the lender. So, it is important to make sure that the application form is correctly completed and that all information provided is true and accurate. You must inform your mortgage lender promptly when there are unexpected changes to your personal or financial status. This includes changes to the marital, income, or work statuses.

Chapter 16: Decks

This is a thorny subject. The lifespan of a deck will depend on the geographic location, maintenance and exposure to sunlight. In general, an well-maintained deck can last for 20 years, however it may fail earlier based on the conditions mentioned above.

Composite decking has gained popularity in recent years. However, it is important to be aware that this type of material will scratch, fade and even warp. As with all new materials that is available composite decking is continuing to develop and can be a distinct difference between the low and high quality materials. When this material first hit on the scene, it was advertised as low maintenance. Manufacturers are now claiming it to be low maintenance. Regarding how long they'll last in the long run, the jury is out on the issue. It is certain that composite decking is more durable than wood, however it may not be a permanent fixture.

There are many elements within your home that could be outdated before they become functionally outdated. Cabinetry, flooring countertops, and cabinets have longevity, however styles come and go out of style.

Even if a piece of equipment in your home is nearing to the close of the normal lifespan, does not mean that it needs to be replaced. I've come across some old appliances that performed better than others right off from the floor of production. However, there are few consumers today who would like an avocado green refrigerator.

Certainly, many of the items listed will last past the expected lifespan especially if they've been maintained and cleaned regularly. The one thing I'd like to warn you about is not replacing the heater. If a hot water heater is damaged, it could cause serious damage. The signs the tank's performance is failing are corrosion of the water, a decrease in efficiency, and a loud banging or rumbling sounds emanating from the appliance.

Make an amount for a budget

The majority of what I'm about to discuss in the next chapters is going to take some time and cleaning materials. However, to be competitive in your market you might need to put aside some cash. Therefore, let's talk about the budget and priority areas.

Armed with your list of punches of the things that should be addressed to make your home more competitive on the market as well as your home inspection it's time to begin to figure things out.

I worked with a wonderful buyer who had acquired a house from her aunt. I was invited to visit and offer suggestions. She had $2,000 available and was allowing herself three months to get her home checked to sell. The counter-top in the kitchen and sink had been damaged and needed replacing. The floor was outdated, but it was still in good shape and was clean. I helped her select the counter top that matched the blue dust in the flooring, and also an idea for a painting sample on the wall. I was contacted in panic when the contractor arrived to put in the counter. He suggested she seriously consider putting in a new flooring.

If there was no money to spend I'd be adamant about putting on a new floor. However, in reality, we could do with the flooring and the addition of a counter as well as the matching paint made it appear like it was designed to be used in the kitchen. I asked my client "does contractors install flooring?" She said he did. I informed her that I thought the contractor was seeking more money for his pay. Take receipts as well as maintenance records, owner's manuals.

Nothing exudes pride of ownership quite like the appearance of a binder or folder with proof of having taken care of your home. An excellent item to have in your possession is a log that documents the HVAC (Heating Ventilating and Cooling) maintenance. Because home inspectors generally aren't usually certified in HVAC they often suggest that buyers have their

HVAC system cleaned and inspected. This is primarily to ensure that the inspector is protected however, buyers can be worried. If you've had the HVAC system cleaned and inspected prior to putting your property for sale and you are able to get around the issue altogether. It is possible to build a stronger case by proving that you've been able to keep the HVAC regularly maintained over time.

If you perform the maintenance yourself, record a journal of when the work was completed and when they're due to be done.

Each buyer has read the numerous upgrades that the seller has listed. Nothing can prove the money that you've put into your house more than receipts of the work and materials that went into your house.

In your binder for maintenance, there must be the owner's manuals of the appliances that you use in your home. I've seen homes where the oven appeared been built in 1950. Inside, in a drawer is the owner's guide.

What should you do if aren't able to find these items? Don't worry. It's not an issue even if you don't have these items. But, when you go through the cleaning process, you might be surprised by how many of these items pop up! In addition numerous manuals can be downloaded from the internet. You can also include a link to the manual inside your binder.

De-Cluttering

Stuff. It seems like things just pile up and the longer you've lived in your house the more likely you will be to own more than your fair share of things. Many people find that having to manage their belongings is a an excuse to put off moving. The best part about cleaning your home is that when moving day arrives you will have plenty less to take care of.

How do you go about eating an elephant? One bite at each time!

Studies have shown that the best amount of time spent in any given task is about 25 minutes, then a five minute break. After that, you may return to your task or shift to another task. A time limit grants you the right to begin and also a commitment to complete. If you can combine these increases and can really help you get rid of the list of tasks.

Get rid of the monster. There's always a part of your home that's large, ugly mess you're anxious about having to clean up. It should be your primary priority. If you do not manage to get the area you live into, you'll be contemplating it, and giving it too much power. However, once the beast has been tamed and tamed, smaller projects will go through.

Before you move on, figure out the location of your beast. If you're a clean person, it could just be an item in your drawer. Perhaps, you be a colossal house from top to the bottom. No worries. I'll guide you through the steps step-by-step.

Donate - Trash- Store Re-incorporate

The four items you'll do with your belongings.

Donate: Selling off your house is a wonderful opportunity to take a break from a multitude of belongings you've kept. There's also plenty of great nonprofit organizations that could benefit from your possessions. If you file an itemized tax return can also be benefited.

There are many organizations that will not accept furniture or clothes. However, with a bit of study, you'll be able to locate the best place to donate your belongings. It could be beneficial to find families through your church or an group that's looking for your goods. Women's shelters often accept bedding and clothes.

You might also look into selling your items through Craig's list or on EBay. Be sensible. If you've never had the opportunity to sell anything on these platforms and are trying to sell it while you are getting your house ready for sale might not be the best right time to start learning.

Also, set things aside for friends and family members you are certain they'd like and will be able to take possession of within the next week.

Trash. If it's damaged, stained, or has missing pieces, discard it. It is inevitable that you will regret throwing it out. However, keeping the items you no longer need can decrease the amount of storage space available to your home and make your house appear tiny, which is why we know smaller homes are sold for hundreds of dollars less than large homes that have plenty with storage. Before you claim that a space that is packed with a lot of things will show how much room your house has there is nothing further than the way that buyers see the space.

If you're still not convinced take into consideration that based on the items, locations and how much you've stored away, your possessions could result in a fire at your home or be a danger to potential buyers who are visiting your house.

Store. There are items you wish to keep however, in order for your home to present in the best way, they must be taken away from the house. This is the kind of stuff that you must store away from the site. The best location to store these items is in the homes of family or friends members. If they are able to spare a space in their attic, basement or an extra room, this is an excellent alternative.

Be upfront about how much space you will need. Be very careful about the items you keep. Make a promise to be aggressive with your pricing and strategic in your staging to are able to sell your house quickly. Your agent will be able to give you the average number of days on the market. This can give you an approximate estimate of how many days you could have to keep things. Return your possessions after the review. Don't let the items you have as a guest at a home who doesn't respect their guests.

The other alternative is a paid storage facility off-site. It can be a fantastic quick fix. But, it comes with the cost of. The cost of storage space varies depending on location, size and whether it's climate-controlled. There are also penalties for any damage that is caused to the unit. So ensure you're careful when it comes to how much you keep and how fast you move your items around.

Be aware of your requirements prior to making a decision to purchase a space, to ensure that you buy the right unit for the things you're storing. If you're storing things which you'll require frequent access to, then you'll be required to ensure the space you are renting is adequate space to move about.

Check with your insurance provider for homeowners to find out if you're able to obtain insurance for the things. There may be a need for an additional rider to protect storage insurance.

To protect your possessions to prevent melting snow and torrential downpours as well as leakage through other systems, you should consider keeping your items off the floor using pallets. Also, I suggest you wrap your items with plastic. This will stop creatures and dust that love to squish themselves into objects from getting in your treasured objects. Be aware of items that are vulnerable to cold or heat temperatures. Certain things are secured from the elements while others aren't. If you are unsure, err to the side of keeping your treasured items protected.

Draw the area. Create a diagram in a plastic cover in the door that will show you where and what the things you have stored. Label all the boxes. Even with a fantastic diagram it's difficult to remember what's in the boxes.

Don't put an empty storage container on your property. Nothing says "we do not have enough space in our house," like a storage container next to your home.

If you are able to stage and price your home correctly the home is likely to be sold quickly and the property will not require storage for the duration of time.

Chapter 17: Professional Tips For

The First Impression

As an owner the first of your duties is to give tenants a secure high-quality, well-lit space to reside. As a result of providing a safe and a high-quality space, you will earn an income per month through rent and, if they're exceptionally well-behaved tenants, they'll be able to be able to do so with the least amount of hassle to you. The most effective method to locate those tenants is to have your property's assets highlighted. This isn't just for prospective tenants but also for other tenants, including insurance inspectors.

Inspections for insurance usually occur at different intervals during renting. The inspector should be sure that the property is in good working order. The majority of insurance companies will check the premises after the policy is in place and every couple of years thereafter.

If you think about it If you were an insurance company, would you be willing to cover a building which was not maintained properly? Most likely not. In some instances you might think that this property was a lawsuit just waiting to happen, and this is the last thing that the insurance company and landlord would want to occur.

Here are a few items an insurance agent could be looking over:

Was the address exactly as stated on the application form by the insurance agent? Is the address right?

Does it appear like it was designed in the time it was mentioned within the app?

Are the area and number of units listed on the application corresponding to what was in the application?

Do you have your housekeeping up to par? In particular is the driveway clear of potholes that are just waiting for claims? Are the trees kept or sit in the air (causing additional roof damage and possibly leaks)?

Are the rental units vacant or occupied? Insurance policies that are preferred will only allow a specified percent (20-35 percent) of vacant spaces at a period of. If the property is vacant, there could be more damage in the event an water leak or someone causing damage to the building and not being noticed for a long period of duration. (See Chapter 21 for "Vacant" property).

Each of these things are to aid the owner in to avoid the possibility of a claim. A poor housekeeping record also affects the kind of tenant and the way in which the property is managed and the likelihood of the possibility of a claim.

Let's discuss the property it self. Before you rent, you'll typically paint and do any repairs needed to make your property prepared.

Other considerations to make when updating your property:

Make sure you choose timeless and long-lasting changes that are timeless and durable. Although it's tempting to keep up with the latest trends in home decor It is best to keep your home's decor simple and timeless. Before you purchase new flooring or lighting fixtures consider, "Will this still look good five or ten years in the future?" Go for neutral colors and sturdy clean-up-friendly finishes.

Select the carpeting. Do you intend to change the flooring every tenant or do you think a lighter color ceramic or wood tile be most effectively? While it might cost more than carpet installation however, it will not need to be replaced. If the worst case scenario occurs the tenant falls and drops something weighty on the floor, it would be possible to fix the damaged area rather than re-carpeting the entire area. Additionally, lighter-colored ceramic tiles or wood help to make the room appear larger when displaying the property to rental. For pet owners it could be a huge advantage over carpets.

Maintain the cooling and heating systems current and well-maintained. There could be an unpleasant smell emanating from the unit that is cooling. It could be caused by filthy or blocked coils that may not just cause the undesirable smell, but limit air flow. The unit is forced to be more efficient, which in turn makes it less efficient, but also reducing its lifespan as well. It is important to have your handyman clean the air filter inside this unit at least three times a year to keep this from happening. It is likely that your tenant isn't likely to worry about changing air filters.

Improve the landscaping. The planting of perennials and hardscaping can require minimal effort, however, they can make a big impact. Hardscaping refers to the process of placing harder materials around the yard. It includes decks, patios and fire pits, as well as rock gardens, and other structures which don't have plants. With the proper amount of space and style the yard will be stunningly attractive. For the back yard, it could also be very practical as fire pits and decks are a great option for tenants. Because you're taking more space by using harder materials such as stone, wood or concrete and concrete, the amount of work you'll need to do in the surroundings is reduced.

Create a welcoming entrance - A low-cost, but worthwhile investment is to make the front of your home or apartment attractive. Making changes to the exterior door will make a big impact. If you are thinking of a new front door, required, mailboxes of high quality windows that are functional and look great and more. If you live in an area that is vulnerable to natural disasters think about weather-related windows as well as the extent to which they improve the value of your home. It will be the tenant's first impression, and first impressions can go far.

Maintain a schedule of regular cleaning of your gutters as well as trimming the trees, and keeping debris away from the structure, as well with other regular items. It is worth considering including artificial grass. It is regarded as being green because it doesn't require fertilizer, water or mowing. Artificial grass is among the most economical, long-term solutions for a neat lawn that needs the minimum amount of maintenance. It is a bit more costly at the beginning of installation, but you should not consider this for sprawling, massive fields. Furthermore, the most recent artificial grass is attractive enough to trick people into believing that it's actually real.

Replace baseboards as required, since damaged or scratched baseboards can be affordable and easy to replace.

The replacement of knobs or handles can be a simple way to make your home more modern. Replace the old knobs on your door and handles for kitchen cabinets with modern ones.

Record the improvements and repairs for the building. It seems like a simple task but it can prove that you're ahead in the curve and are taking the best care of both you and your tenants.

Perform a thorough clean or ask a service to complete the task for you. Make sure you pay particular attention to dust accumulation on the ceiling as well as furnace vents, among other places that aren't normally part of the regular cleaning of your units.

Note: If the insurance company has an inspector report about the property, they'll provide the owner with a report detailing the requirements for repairs as well as other suggestions. Be sure to reply and make the necessary repairs. If you don't then, you won't remain with the preferred insurance provider.

Another option that we suggest is to solicit comments from tenants on their opinions on what they like and do not appreciate about the home. The majority of tenants are willing to share their opinions about what they believe should be changed or updated. Imagine yourself in the shoes of a tenant. What would you like to be to be fixed if you lived there? Keep in mind that you the landlord are the ones who take the decision-making, not your tenants.

Remember that every person's preferences differ. You can see from your neighbors often what's acceptable in landscape colors, colors of paint and more. Be careful not to be too prominent. You do not want to be the neighbour with the yellow home and the landscape that has become the talking point of the neighborhood.

Chapter 18: Probate Real Estate

Probate is the lawful procedure that allows the estate of a deceased person is administered. Probate is the lawful way to transfer assets, such as homes, vehicles and bonds, stocks boats, personal belongings that were in the deceased person's name into the estate of the deceased so that they can be distributed or sold to the inheritors.

If a person dies and has assets in greater than $100,000, their estate has to go through probate. The process is overseen and controlled by the probate court.

If the decedent has an estate plan that specifies the way in which his or her estate is to be divided after the death of the decedent, the probate court will decide if the will should be allowed to probate and be given legal effect. If the deceased person dies without leaving a will, the court will appoint the Personal Representative to disperse the property of the deceased in accordance with the laws of descent and distribution. These laws govern the distribution of assets based upon the hereditary succession.

Real Estate could be part of an estate. In some cases, the real estate is by the owner in full and undisputed possession, but at in other instances, the property could be subject to the mortgage. The probate-related property includes condos, homes or timeshares, a lot of land, as well as commercial properties.

If there is a Personal Representative or Executor is named , it's their responsibility to collect deedsand insurance papers, mortgage and annuity documents. The representative also has the responsibility to secure the assets during probate, and to liquidate them according to the wishes of the deceased, or as needed to settle outstanding debts.

When a person, or an estate decides to sell their property and what is the best way to do it? Depends on the state of the property or the urgency at which funds are required the most effective methods for liquidation is either selling through an agent, or by contacting an investor cash buyer.

In some instances the court may require the sale to be fair market and the sale could require or not require court approval. If the approval of the court is required the court will request an independent appraisal to provide an indication of the value. The guideline used will form the base for the list price and, even after the offer is accepted the sale could still be subject to overbids.

In most cases the court's approval is needed when there is a concern that the sale price isn't an accurate representation of the an actual market price. In this kind of case is protecting an interest of a third party that may have invested an interest in the result of the sale. In the event of probate it could be that there is a mortgage on the house or it could be other debts to be paid out of the estate.

To prevent any appearance of impropriety or to avoid any other secret agreements to avoid the appearance of fraud, listing agents generally require offers to be sealed in an envelope with a check for 10 percent of the price of the purchase. The offers will be scrutinized and the best price will be chosen. The final selection is subject to the approval of the court.

This system safeguards the clients from unscrupulous agents who could be collaborating with investors or friends to buy the house for less than fair market value, and later report to the trustee of bankruptcy that there were no offers were made.

If court approval is needed The court will then confirm the sale of the real estate to the bidder who originally made the offer or an over bidder in the confirmation hearing of the court. The hearing can be attended by the general public, and can have interested persons attending the bid may be an overbid by another buyer. The bid should be much greater than the original bid. If a bid that is higher than the original one accepts, then the bidder must bring cash or a valid check in order to be recognized as the bidder with the highest amount.

If there are more than one bidder or if the initial bidder would like to bid more than the initial overbid, they will be given the option to raise their bid during the hearing for confirmation. The amount of bid increment that is required following the first overbid is determined in the hands of the judge. The court will consider bids in the exact way as auctions up to the point that the most expensive bid is presented during an auction confirmation.

If probate property is an estate Trust Sale or if the Executor or Administrator of the estate is given "full independent power" in accordance with the Independent Administration of Estates Act (IAEA) the sale is not required to have court approval. If the Administrator is granted full independence, he or can decide to put up the property as a sale. After an offer has been accepted by the estate's attorney, the attorney sends out an Notice of Proposed Action stating the terms of the sale proposed to all heirs in the event that there are more. The heirs have 15 days to contest the sale. If there isn't any objection after 15 calendar days the auction is allowed to go without a court hearing needed.

Sometimes, an Executor or the inheriting party is not in a good the state of. If the property's condition is considered to be excellent or better than the asset could most likely be liquidated to get the highest amount of money through contacting a probate Realtor.

A Probate attorney can help the estate over a far away by offering additional services by forming an experienced team of professionals. By team, I'm talking about trash removal specialists, such as cleaners, haulers, liquidators, movers, etc. . The agent will have the property cleaned for a minimal costand will then offer the property for sale at the fair market value.

What happens if an inherited or probate property requires repairs? If it's an approved by the court and a qualified appraiser has assessed the property, the price of repairs could be subtracted in the amount of fair market value.

If the sale doesn't need court approval or confirmation, the estate may choose for the sale of the home to investors or cash buyers who can flip houses. You will get less cash from a cash buyer , but you can't fix up a home for a probate sale in order to make an attempt to sell the property for more cash.

In California probate, properties are offered "as-is." When you do repairs, you could be unaware of something concerning the state that the house is in. A simple coat of paint may accidentally cover up a problem. Apart from removing personal belongings or trash, as well as clearing the entrance and the yard, it's crucial for the house to be in the current state . Then, let the prospective buyers conduct their own inspections and be satisfied with what is happening to the house.

A Probate Realtor who is experienced knows this, and it could help you avoid some liabilities later.

If the house was being used as a rental, or the family member or a member of the estate were living there then you might be able to make some repairs.

Chapter 19: Adverts Running to Purchase Property

In addition to the strategies I've been teaching you I want you to be able to create ads that bring in those who are looking to sell their house to you. It's free to select a location to try. The strategy I'll discuss with you will make your phone to ring. Let's go.

Test the Market Online

If you're thinking that a market may be a good one and provide certain opportunities but you're not certain it's best to try it out and see what you think.

To try it out for free it is possible to visit sites similar to Craigslist and use it to check out what's available to see how many individuals are looking to sell their house and see how many have inventory they're trying to sell. You'll get:

* Investors
* Homeowners and
* People who inherit properties.

You'll be able to hear all the various tales and motivations for why they'd like to make a sale, and it's free of any money.

I even placed an advertisement on Craigslist that reads:

We're hoping to purchase 50
properties located in the region. We're Accepting applications for
the first 200 people who are who are looking for a way to sell.

Call us at 1-800-555-1212 today.

Make it seem urgent. Everyone else on the market has advertisements that say, "WE BUY HOUSES." It's not very appealing. It's essential to convey a sense of urgency. It should be as simple as ... The company is hoping to acquire 50 homes over the weekend, by Sunday or we'll need to purchase 85 properties. A campaign like this one will make the phone ring off the line.

It's a fantastic way to you to check out the market. If people call you to buy a house You're in a position of authority because they're asking you to market their house.

This method will allow you to develop your expertise in the field, and at no cost.

If they call you when they call you, tell them: "What's the best case scenario?" "What are you planning to sell this property on?"

Use words that contain embedded commands like, delete this property clear from this property.

Use phrases such as: "If you could get the money in just 24 hours then what would you sell it for now?"

If they say, "Well, I'm not planning to sell the property," you respond by declaring, "Oh, well if I could cash out within 24 hours, how much would that amount of money cost?" Or, you might say, "I don't know anything about the neighborhood. Wow, that's a lot of high."

If you are being called by people to make a phone call, it is an excellent opportunity (advantage) to sit at the wheel. tell them:

* "Well I'd like to see photos."
* "What kind of property is it?"
* "How many bedrooms?"
* "How many bathrooms?"

This is the best method to check out the market and have clients calling . Then you can apply the strategies I described earlier to assess the market value and ensure you are receiving a good price.

It's also possible to make the same type of advertisement in local newspapers, however you'll be charged a small amount for the advertisement. I'd rather go to the Internet. I've seen numerous advertisements in local newspapers for houses to buy and sell houses. Instead of putting the street signs all over that make people angry and people angry because you're placing these on the fence or their poles on the street or on their street poles, you can target an appropriate audience by putting your advertisement online. This is your target audience people who are seeking to sell their house.

The advantages of selling online

The majority of times, it sells faster. Do not take a minimum of 60 days before selling by a realtor

* You'll save the cost of selling and buying commissions since it's not through an agent

* You're not waiting two months to close the deal after you've signed a contract for the property.

* Online does have more coverage and the potential for an interest in the property.

Selling online can be accomplished from your home, with less effort.

The Market by distributing letters

Instead of selling through the internet certain people mail letters to customers. It's 49 cents per letter, however it's great.

Let me share an example. I found a Medical School located in a prime location only two blocks from the major University. I decided to distribute notices to all those within the range of these two universities. The cost was not any money. It's just a $200 investment to see if there's some great deals. I emailed owners of hundreds around these two colleges.excellent bargains and I sent hundreds of owners around these two colleges.excellent bargains and I sent to hundreds of owners in these two colleges.excellent bargains and I sent out to hundreds of owners in the vicinity of these two colleges.

If someone responds to my email and then calls me back, I inform them the same things I advised you to those Craigslist users. Examples include "You are aware that I've wrote all these letters and am trying to find something appealing at the university However, I'm in need of the deal to be logical financially."

* "I have cash readily available and I'm prepared to make a deal."

* "What cost is it going to cost me if I make you money fast?"

They can respond:

"Well God I'll offer you a fantastic price if we close on time. I'm tired of having to deal with this home."

And I'll say: "Well I did get lots of inquiries from these letters. What is the number at the bottom you'll use in this particular property?"

I could just be able to say:

"You are being fair , and I agree with the conditions."

At an epoch, you'll need to answer:

"You are being rational. You're not insane. I'll try that. When can I go and see the property. If they offer you an extremely high price, do not hesitate to bargain with them based on their comps in the vicinity. Condition is a factor with it, so make sure to take that into consideration. Get pictures, as I have mentioned earlier."

If you're outside the region, you could declare:

"You know I'm not in town at the moment or I reside near (fill your own) however, I do have a person from the area nearby who will be available to visit."

You'll need to locate someone local who would be able to visit wherever you are.

You can contact the owner currently. Try to say something like:

"This could happen much quicker if you can snap a few photos today and send me the pictures. Use your mobile phone and snap me some photos. I don't care if the home is clean or dirty. I'm not interested in the dirt. I'm only trying to figure out what we're discussing. I've driven past your house however I've never been inside."

The business's critics might be like, "Oh my gosh! You're going to mail an email? You're going through the hassle?"

It's basically a formal letter. It's a matter of sending it to the postal office. Here's an example of the letter I use to implement this method:

Sample Form Letter

Dear Neighbor,

We're new in the region and am interested in purchasing a home in your area. If you're looking to sell your house, contact me.

I have cash in my account and have the ability to pay you right away. Give me a call and let me know if or anyone you know, is looking to sell their home.

I am not a real estate agent or broker. If we are able to come to a mutual understanding and agree to a mutually acceptable agreement, there won't be an waiting period for escrow or commissions for real estate brokers. This way, it will be beneficial for us both.

I'll only be in town for a couple of days, and I'd be grateful for a prompt response. I can be reached directly by dialing 805-555-1212. If I'm not available you can leave a message and I'll return your call as soon as possible.

Best of luck,

When I first started out in real estate around twelve years ago, signed with an older man who had more than 30 years of buying real estate expertise. He was a master of buying properties at a price at a price that was below the market. He was not very good at selling his properties. In fact, when I first met him, he had 42 properties. I was in business for a couple of months and was learning to acquire excellent properties at a reasonable price from him.

I was proficient at selling homes, but I realized that the lower the market value I bought this property the greater profit I earned when I was able to sell it. I was curious about how he managed to buy a house for such a low price. I learned everything that he could about this industry, and 12 years later, I'm able present a more sophisticated version of what I learned while working together with the man for 9 months.

It is important to note that I gained lots of things when working with his. I also learned some things that I did not want to do because they didn't match my notion of integrity and how I would like being treated. This is an illustration of what I do not do when purchasing properties.

Our ad was published in the newspaper. The same ad ran for several years. It would receive several calls per day, and possibly five calls per day. One day, he's saying, "Hey, Mike, I received a call which sounds like a great bargain. Let's head out to check if we have an interesting deal." I replied, "Okay. Let's go."

As we approach the home, I'm thinking: Wow, beautiful woodwork, fantastic detail and a large lot. I'm excited. I'm thinking"Wow, if she's asking $8,000 or $10,000 as she said during the call I'm sure I could make a profit selling it for $30,000-$40,000. $40,000. It's going to be an absolute nightmare. It's just an instant flip and we'll be out and in.

Its owner is lovely elderly lady. It must have been her home for over a long period of time because she claimed she was going to a nursing home. She was very charming. My friend says to my partner "Mike take a look at this. We're planning to purchase this house."

He asks, "Do you know what you're planning to sell the property on?"

The lady responds, "Oh, gosh, you know, if you could earn $8,000 it would be amazing." This was the lowest part of the estimate she offered when she called.

It's like: My god that's $8,000! I'm willing to accept the conditions "as as" I believe she was honest and giving us an a very good price. I'm prepared to go into the nearest bank to collect cash, and make the deal.

My partner responds, "No way. For this piece of junk I'd never offer the amount of $2,000."

I'm thinking: What? Are you crazy?

She sat for a few minutes and then states, "Okay."

He smiles when she's not watching.

I'm wondering: What is going on? That's ridiculous. We're sure to make profits at the asking price, by selling the property to an international audience. The property was valued at around $10,000, when we rented the property out and put in some cosmetics, we could earn a decent return. It's not necessary to squeeze the little lady so difficult. Don't be so hard on her. What she gave us was a fantastic bargain for us, without having to negotiate . However, if she needed to engage an agent, pay for the commissions and an attorney to finish the deal, she'd have to wait for months and only get about 10k once all the payments were made, therefore it was reasonable for her to earn 8k to move on, and it was far more fair for us.

The point is that I'm not going to tell her, "Oh, your $8,000 is too low, so let's increase it to $10,000." However, in the same way I'm not going convince her that it's not worthy of the amount she asked for since it's not my way to tell people lies to make a profit. It's fine to say that the highest amount I'll accept is X dollars but it's not appropriate to make up a story about the worth of something when that it's not the truth.

If someone tells me they'd like $20,000 and I reply that I'd like to spend $12,000, I'm not saying that it's not worth the amount of $20,000. I'll say to them "I cannot make more money than 12 000." I'm not going to be lying and claim it's worth more than the amount. I'll just tell them the price I'd be willing to pay. I was so sorry for her. My partner was just smiling. I've learned a lot from this incident about why I was not interested in doing business.

Running ads are a fantastic Method to Find Amazing Deals!

* You can place advertisements via the Internet.

* You can also call advertisements via the Internet.

* You can mail letters.

* You could even make those annoying signs.

I'm offering my personal perspective. I'm not attempting to put posters all over the neighborhood with my number, and that say "CALL me." It's likely receive angry calls from people who will call you with questions such as, "Why is this sign on my fence? Why is it placed on this lamppost?" You'll get city inspectors calling to say, "You can't post your signs on telephone poles, fences or on streetlights."

It's clear that advertising to buy properties is a great method. Some people believe that this could be successful. Aren't all people doing it? But you do it in a different way. It's not like you throw advertisements that read "WE Buy Houses" throughout the neighborhood , and then think that you're the first to do it. Consider different approaches and ways to make your phone ring. Make it happen in so that people are interested in doing business with you.

Conclusion

Thank you for getting all the way to the conclusion of this guide, let's hope it's useful and capable of providing you with the tools needed to reach your goals, regardless of what they are.

It is the next thing to do, which is determine which type of real estate investment you'd like to pursue. There are a myriad of possibilities available for those who want to begin however it takes some time and effort. This book takes an overview of the aspects involved in buying real estate, and what you must do to begin. From selecting a great property to obtaining the funds that will allow you to make a profit by engaging with a professional real estate professional as well as protecting your investments and establishing leases should you choose to invest in rental properties, you're certain to be able to master all you require to know to begin your journey into real estate investing now!